YOUR BEST NAP NOW

Martha Bolton

YOUR BEST NAP NOW

7 Steps to Nodding Off
at Your **Full Potential**

BETHANYHOUSE
MINNEAPOLIS, MINNESOTA

Published by Bethany House Publishers
11400 Hampshire Avenue South
Bloomington, Minnesota 55438

Bethany House Publishers is a division of
Baker Publishing Group, Grand Rapids, Michigan.

Printed in the United States of America

Library of Congress Cataloging-in-Publication Data

Bolton, Martha.
    Your best nap now : 7 steps to nodding off at your full potential / Martha Bolton.
        p.   cm.
    Summary: "Comedienne Martha Bolton mixes humorous anecdotes about life after
fifty with touching stories about what life's all about to help ease the way through middle
age"—Provided by publisher.
ISBN 978-0-7642-0309-1 (pbk. : alk. paper) 1. Aging—Humor. I. Title.

    PN6231.A43B657   2009
    814'.54—dc22

                                                                        2008051212

To Evelyn . . .
a friend with endless encouragement and impeccable timing.

ABOUT THE AUTHOR

Martha Bolton is a full-time comedy writer and author of more than fifty books, including *Didn't My Skin Used to Fit?* She was a staff writer for Bob Hope for fifteen years and has also written for Phyllis Diller, Wayne Newton's USO show, Ann Jillian, Jeff Allen, and many other entertainers. Her writing has appeared in *Reader's Digest, Chicken Soup for the Soul,* and *Brio* magazine. She has received four Angel Awards and an Emmy nomination. She and her husband live in Tennessee.

Contents

STEP 1: ENLARGE YOUR FONT

The Universal Language 15

Living in My Jeans. 18

Is There a Doctor in the Hardware Section? 20

Self-Help Books for Middle-Agers and Beyond 23

Happy 150th Birthday to Me! 24

The Changing of the Words. 26

Lifetime Achievement Awards 27

STEP 2: DEVELOP A HEALTHY OBLIVION

Your Best Nap Now 33

Breaking News 41

Enjoying the Peace and Quiet 44

Ten Advantages to Global Warming (For the
    Middle-Aged Person) 46

Ten Stupid Things Middle-Aged Women Do to Mess
    Up Their Lives 47

Second-Childhood Board Games. 48

A "Wait" Problem. 52

STEP 3: DISCOVER THE POWER OF YOUR REGRETS AND WHINING

What Were We Thinking? 57

What Chocolate Dreams May Come. 59

Ten Things a Menopausal Woman Should Never Do. 61

Women and Politics. 62

The Housing Slump. 65

They Don't Write Them Like They Used To. 69

The New/Old Fall Season 71

Times Change 74

Best Friends of Young and Old Alike. 76

Duly Warned. 79

Hurry Up! 81

Retirement Pros and Cons. 84

STEP 4: LET GO OF THE PORK CHOP

The Over-Fifty Diet Plan 89

Daily Workouts. 93

Pass the Toxins, Please. 95

Eating Our Way to Youth 97

One Lump or Two? 99

St. John's Dessert Tray. 101

Having Your Cake and Eating It, Too 104

STEP 5: FIND STRENGTH IN COVER CREAM

Trendsetting Boomers 109

Fashion Faux Pas. 112

I've Got the Music in Me. 115

The Saggy Sisters Society. 117

No More Ducking. 120

At Long Last Love. 122

Beauty Tips on the Cheap 124

STEP 6: LIVE TO ANNOY

Red Tape 129

Smart Chips . . . and Dip 132

The Baby Boomer's "How Long Will You Live?" Test 135

Son, Can I Borrow the Car? 137

Bickering Could Be Hazardous to Your Health 141

Calling All Grouches 144

They're Baaaaaack! 147

STEP 7: CHOOSE TO KEEP GOING

Ten Money-Saving Tips for Today's Economy 153

How High Will It Go? 156

A Matter of Will 158

Survivors 162

Letters to Old Friends 164

Those Three Little Words 166

Plenty of Time Left 168

Stretching Our Days 170

We Could All Use a Hero 173

Living Life in Reverse 176

Taking Inventory 178

Lost and Found 180

High Tea, Bowling, and Other Family Traditions 183

Longevity 185

Next Chapters 187

Consciousness: That annoying time between naps.

(seen on a bumper sticker)

STEP ONE:

Enlarge Your Font

The Universal Language

"United we stand, divided we fall."
Patrick Henry
"And without our glasses we see nothing at all."
Martha Bolton

There has been a lot of debate over which translation of the Bible is the most accurate. Some people insist that it is the King James Version, while others are equally convinced that one of the more modern translations is most accurate. Their reasoning is that since modern English is easier to comprehend, it leaves less room for errors of interpretation.

However, more and more biblical scholars are beginning to come to a different conclusion, the same one that I reached some years ago. Unequivocally, the most accurate translation of the Bible is *Large Print*.

In fact, after the age of fifty, the most accurate version of anything is the one in large print. If you've ever tried to read a map or the fine print on a bottle of medicine, you know what I'm talking about.

Thankfully, publishers and some pharmaceutical companies are answering this need by bringing out more books, magazines, newspapers, and pharmaceutical instructions in bigger fonts. Even some restaurants now provide large-print versions of their menus.

I believe the retiring baby boomer generation is driving this movement. Never before has there been such a crowd of people hitting retirement age at one time. Many companies are just now realizing this sizeable marketing demographic exists.

We need to realize it, too. *We have power, people!* Think of how many changes we could get made in society if we would just pool our resources and our energies. We are not our parents' generation. We want to live differently in our retirement. We don't want to sit in our rocking chairs and watch the neighbors—and our lives—go by. Not that there's anything wrong with a sedentary lifestyle. I'm planning on incorporating a little "sedentary" into my own lifestyle someday. There's a rocking chair somewhere with my name on it, and I'm going to spend a lot of time rocking it into a pile of splinters when the time comes.

But I'm not ready for that assignment yet. Right now I've got too much to see and do. And one of the things I enjoy doing is *seeing*. And when the print is larger, it makes that process so much easier.

So thanks, Bible publishers, for offering us large print. Thanks, *Reader's Digest* and other magazines, for enlarging your fonts, too. Thanks, map creators, for supersizing your print so that I've ended up in Cleveland, where I had intended to go, and not Charleston, which wasn't in my travel plans at that time. Thanks, pharmaceutical companies, for making your instructions a little easier to read so I take my medicines as prescribed. After all, there is a huge difference between "Take two pills" and "Make two pies." (Frankly, I prefer the latter, but that probably won't do a lot to help my thyroid.)

English, Spanish, German, French, and every other tongue on the earth—they all have their beauty. But I'm holding on to hope that one day soon, Large Print will be the universal language.

Living in My Jeans

I bought a new pair of jeans the other day, but there is a problem. It's not that I don't like them. I do. They're a good fit and they're stylish. The problem is, I'm not all that fond of their brand name. I won't share it here because I don't want to cast the company in a bad light. Like I said, they do make a very good product. But their name isn't something I want embroidered across my hips. It isn't the name of a well-known designer like Gloria Vanderbilt or Versace. It's not a cool name like 7 For All Mankind or even Lucky.

Their brand name is, well, it's a type of building. That's right— *a building*. I won't say what kind of building—again, so I don't embarrass the company. But I will give you a hint. It's something like Condo. Now I ask you, would you really want to wear a pair of jeans that has the word Condo written on the back pocket?

What's next? Arena? Or Coliseum (spoken with an Italian accent, of course)? Spacious Estates?

Is the day coming when we'll have to buy our jeans from draftsmen, who'll design our fit and then have to submit their plans to our city's building committee? Will we one day see "Frank Lloyd Wright" jeans? Will they do away with sizes like 8, 10, and 12, and make us buy our jeans by square footage? Or acreage? If we buy a matching top, would that be considered adding a second story? If someone borrows our jeans, is that trespassing?

And what about the boomer generation? Are they going to design a pair of jeans specifically for those senior men who prefer wearing their waistband closer to their armpits, and call them High Rises?

Where will it end?

We didn't have this problem when the clothing simply said Sears or JCPenney, and their tag was tucked neatly behind our necks or waists. But now designers are sticking these names all over us, turning us into their walking billboards.

I'll go along with it for now because, like I said, I do like the jeans. They're comfortable and roomy, and they sort of do feel like "home." So maybe that's the reason for the name.

But if jeans start coming with an address, or someone starts a jeans company called Double-Wides, I'm drawing the property line.

There is one good thing about all of this, I suppose, and that's every time I put on a little weight, I could just pass it off as a "housing bubble."

This story originally appeared on New Christian Voices, *www. newchristianvoices.com/column/marthas-laugh-lines-living-my-jeans,* July 16, 2008.

Is There a Doctor in the Hardware Section?

Surgeons must be very careful,
When they take the knife!
Underneath their fine incisions
Stirs the Culprit—Life!
Emily Dickinson

By now I'm sure you're aware that many drugstores are offering medical treatments at their facilities. That's right—you can now drive to your local pharmacy and get a checkup before you check out. You can even use the express lane if you have ten or fewer procedures done.

Some people are referring to these in-store mini-clinics as "Wal-Docs," and like them or not, they could be the wave of the future.

Personally, I think they're a great idea. How convenient is it to buy all the junk food you want, eat it, and then simply walk to the back of the store and have your arteries unclogged in the same visit?

The only real problem I can see with these drugstore medical clinics is that when they announce "Code Blue" over the PA system, you won't know whether someone is in cardiac arrest in the medical area, or there's a fight going on over discounted Blue's Clues toys in aisle 7.

Still, for anyone who has ever had to sit in a doctor's lobby for countless hours, reading the latest issue of *Bunions Illustrated*, the opportunity to shop while you wait is a welcome concept. So set us free and let us shop until we hear our name called over the loudspeaker. If we have something contagious, they can simply post Caution signs at the end of each aisle, sort of like they do when they've just mopped the floor.

For now, these in-store medical clinics primarily handle minor illnesses and injuries. But who knows what might be available to us in the near future?

"Mrs. Williams, your husband is ready to be picked up in the surgical recovery center on aisle 14," the medical receptionist might announce over the public address system. *"The spleen removal was a success, but you might want to bring one of the larger shopping carts to pick him up, as he's still a little woozy. Oh, and on your way, we'd like to remind you that your vacation prints are ready in the photo department."*

These in-store medical clinics can help speed up your healing, too. If your doctor tells you to put ice on an injury, you'll be able to walk right out of the exam room and go to the freezer section of the store and rest your arm on the stack of Stouffer's frozen entrees. If the recommendation is to get plenty of rest, you can immediately begin doing that in the large pillow bin in the middle of the store. And just imagine: When someone runs over your foot with their shopping cart or a baby carriage, you won't have to stand there hopping on one foot, pretending it didn't hurt. You can get the lacerations immediately attended to, as long as the "doctor is in."

If they ever open up a labor-and-delivery room in these stores, that could get real interesting.

"The pains are still about two minutes apart, Buford. I think we've got time to check out the two-for-one sale going on in the electronics section!"

Talk about shopping till you drop!

With all the overcrowding that's happening at hospitals and doctors' offices today, being able to visit a physician at your local drugstore is probably a good idea.

But if the mammogram machine is ever out of order and the doctor asks you to go to aisle 8 and bring her the waffle iron, that might be your cue to leave.

Self-Help Books for Middle-Agers and Beyond

The Proper Care and Feeding of Your Irritable Bowel Syndrome

Esoterica for the Soul

The Five People You Meet at Denny's

Ten Stupid Things Boomers Do to Mess Up Their DVD Players

Running With Tweezers

The Dummies' Guide to Jeopardy

Who Moved My Social Security Check?

Unleash the Ocean Cruiser Within

The Motor Home Traveler's Gift

The Audacity of Gout

Happy 150th Birthday to Me!

*"I advise you to go on living solely
to enrage those who are paying your annuities.
It is the only pleasure I have left."*
Voltaire

According to some reports, in the not-too-distant future we could feasibly see the average life-span increase to 150 years. That's right. *A hundred and fifty years!* Frankly, I think they keep giving us more time because they know it'll take us that long to save up for our funerals.

But I could be wrong.

Can you imagine living until you're 150 years old? It's an intriguing thought, isn't it? Why, with that much time, there's no telling how much you could accomplish. In the span of 150 years, you:

- might finally get waited on at the DMV.
- could get to see bell bottoms come back into style a couple more times.
- could get an extra fifty years' worth of birthday wishes from Willard Scott.

- could have the satisfaction of knowing that you can still do everything you could do at 120.
- can attend your 125th high school reunion.
- will finally be right-side up on your car lease.
- will finally pay off all that exercise equipment you bought in your thirties but never used.
- could see the cheese in the back of your refrigerator age to 114-year-old perfection.
- will have all-new warranties on most of your replaceable body parts.

This is merely the tip of the iceberg when it comes to the advantages of living to 150 years of age. I haven't even touched on the wisdom that the younger generation (the ninety-year-olds) could glean from all those 150-year-olds!

See, it's a win-win for all of us. But I do think the senior discount should increase after the one-hundred-year mark.

The Changing of the Words

Have you noticed how the meaning of some words change over time? What we called something when we were young may have an entirely different meaning to us as we grow older. Here is just a short list of some words and terms that have changed over time:

What We Called It Then	What We Call It Now
Mood lighting	Power failure
A wink	Dry eye
Friday-night cruising	Looking for a parking space at Walgreens
"Twist and Shout"	Leg cramps
"Hanging Ten"	Outgrowing your orthopedic sandals
Slumber parties	Insomniacs Anonymous meetings
Malibu tan	Age-spot outbreak
Slip 'N Slide	A bubble bath
Greased Lightning	Bengay
Doing donuts in the parking lot	Attacking the Krispy Kremes before you get home

Lifetime Achievement Awards

It's always heartwarming to see someone receive a Lifetime Achievement Award. The recipient of one of these accolades is usually someone very deserving, and the award is long overdue. Most of the time, the reasoning behind the choice of recipients for these awards is clearly recognizable by all.

Lifetime Achievement Awards are given in recognition of many different areas of accomplishment. From the arts to science to politics to you-name-it, trophy houses are kept busy as we honor those whom we deem to be the most praiseworthy.

But what about all the achievers we've overlooked? The people who help us day in and day out but receive little, if any, acknowledgment? Where are their accolades? Where is their praise? Where is their *plaque*?

Exactly.

Before any more time goes by, I would like to take this opportunity to honor those people who have dedicated so much of their time and energy to making our lives a little easier and more rewarding; these heroes who have heretofore gone unnoticed.

- To the genius who invented deep-heating patches, we salute you. Those little wonders allow us to apply the medication directly on the muscle that hurts. (I'm having a dress made out of them myself.) This invention has improved the lives of countless athletes and middle-agers. Or middle-aged athletes. But where is the monument to their inventor? Who is planning his appreciation party? Where is his *plaque*?

- To the men and women who keep vending machines stocked with candies and pretzels, and in some instances, hot soup and coffee, we pay you homage.

    Never mind the fact that the cup usually drops down *after* the coffee has poured forth from the machine. Or the fact that the candy bar doesn't always drop down into the retrieval area and we have to rock the entire machine back and forth until it releases the Snickers, which appears to be holding on for dear life. Never mind that we don't receive our proper change or that the machine itself is out of order three out of the four times we go up to it. These people still deserve our respect. They deserve our thanks. *They deserve a plaque!*

- To the designer of the hospital gown. Sure, we've all heard the jokes, but let's rethink this. Having been repeatedly scolded by his teachers for never finishing anything he started, this man changed medical history when he didn't finish the hospital gown design he was working on. He's made a fortune off his lack of stick-to-itiveness. Doctors love it so much, they've kept the design for dozens of years. But has he ever been given a plaque? No!

- To the servers at all-you-can-eat buffets, who keep the pans and bowls full. They stand at the carving tables, slicing to our liking. They keep the hot rolls coming and tempt us with 114 different kinds of starch. They handle busloads of seniors and high school football teams at a moment's notice. But where's their own appreciation dinner? Where's their applause? *Where's their plaque?*

- To the boxing and bagging boys and box girls who help us out to our car with our groceries. It doesn't matter if it's a 110-degree hot and humid August day or a minus-ten-degree dead-of-winter evening, these shopping-cart angels will load our groceries into our cars, and they'll do it with a smile on their faces. They'll even smile when we can't remember which aisle we parked in. So where's their Hall of Fame? Their tribute? *Their plaque?*

- To the furniture and mattress salesmen who pretend not to notice us taking a nap in their recliners or on their pillowtop mattresses. Without these merciful souls, we would be forced to walk around the store in a stupor, trying our hardest to stay awake amidst all the excitement that goes on in a typical furniture store. (If you're wondering, that was sarcastic.) The only thing less exciting than a furniture store is . . . okay, there's *nothing* less exciting than a furniture store. That's why the salesmen don't complain about our naps. They probably figure it takes the attention off them snoring in the sofa section.

  But are these salesmen ever featured on *Biography*? Only if one of them went berserk and pillow-pummeled a customer to death. That's when they'd get noticed. But they wouldn't get a plaque.

- To the ice-cream scooper who, with no thought to his own safety, risks hand and forearm frostbite to dig single, double, and even triple scoops of this creamy delicacy into our awaiting cones. He doesn't discriminate against us based on our preference for waffle or sugar cone. He merely does his job, day after day, risking his digits and his dignity. (Let's face it, can you really hold your head up while digging out a triple scoop of "tutti-frutti"?)

  But do these gallant men and women ever get recognized for their sacrifice, for the danger they face on a regular basis? Do we applaud them each time they go down into the freezer and start rolling that icy goodness into balls? Have we set up any sort of fund for their next of kin should the unthinkable happen? Has any one of them ever gotten a plaque for service above and beyond the call of duty? Sadly, the answer is no.

- To the Wal-Mart greeters who stand at the ready, cart in hand, saving us from having to separate the carts ourselves. (Who carries that much dynamite with them?) But is there a "Wally" award (the Oscar equivalent for the Wal-Mart greeter) for them? Is there a national holiday designated in his or her honor? Have they, at the very least, ever been given a plaque? Maybe, but I didn't see it on CNN. Did you?

- To the pleasant-voiced man or woman who repeats those precious words, "Please continue to hold, your call will be answered in the order received," and thereby assures us that even though we've been on the line for more than four hours, we're important to the company and they have not forgotten about us. How many times were we just about to hang up when this recording came on, reminding us that we needn't give up hope just yet. Help is on the way. There are only twenty-six more calls ahead of us.

  But has this person behind the voice ever had a banquet held in his or her honor? Has a plaque ever been given? No.

- And finally, to the paperboy who co-partners with so many of us in our exercise programs by hurling our newspapers to out-of-the-way places, such as the roof, the tree, under our car, in our shrubs, and sometimes even directly at us, causing us to keep our reflexes in tip-top shape. Have these fine athletes ever been entered in the Olympics? Have they been considered by major league baseball scouts? Have they ever been given a plaque? You know the answer: no.

It's time to change things. It's time some of these great Americans started being honored. It's time to give credit where credit is due.

It's time to order an awful lot of plaques!

STEP TWO:

Develop a Healthy Oblivion

Your Best Nap Now

"In dog years, I'm dead."

(seen on a T-shirt)

Did you know there are different kinds of naps? I had to extensively research this during the writing of this book, and I was shocked at what I found. For years I was under the assumption that there was only one kind of nap: a one-size-fits-all. It looked the same on everyone—that open-mouth, drool-sliding-down-your-chin, head-flopped-back-in-the-recliner, remote-in-hand kind of nap. But I was mistaken. There are more.

Recognizing the vast variety of naps that are available is why this book was written in the first place. I felt we were stuck in a rut of the same old nap year after year after year. It doesn't have to be that way. Variety is available. But we can't take advantage of all of these naps unless we know about them.

Before we cover the individual naps, though, let's look at the controversy that surrounds the whole napping experience.

It is an accepted fact that babies and toddlers benefit greatly from daily napping. But for some reason we have been led to believe that once we hit adolescence, we outgrow our need for a nap. *Nothing can be further from the truth.*

The desire for a nap never leaves us. It becomes especially evident in our teen years, but our timing gets a little mixed up. We start doing it in history or math class, which is usually frowned upon.

Again, the nap wasn't the problem—it was the timing. But that was never clearly explained to us. So we went through our teenage years believing napping was wrong. We still did it, but our feelings of guilt toward it were obviously misplaced.

Throughout our working years, we found that our inner "napper" was still very much with us, showing up as we fell asleep at our desk after lunch or during our boss's after-dinner speech. Again, we felt remorse. Again, it was misplaced because napping is just a part of being human, and so it wasn't the act of our naps, it was simply the timing of them.

It's no wonder, then, that now, as we move toward our retirement years (and some of us are already there), we find ourselves unable to kick the napping habit.

The fact is, naps are hard-wired into us. Instinctively, we know our bodies need naps to feel revitalized. Naps give us renewed energy and help us make it through the day. They enable us to escape from the afternoon heat or whatever unwelcome task lies before us.

There are so many benefits to the napping experience, we should all cut ourselves some slack and go ahead and reward our bodies with a little midday siesta.

Some people have no problem napping. Politicians nap. How else do you explain some of the bills they pass? Celebrities nap, too. We've all seen movies where the actors seem to have napped their way through their roles. And some drivers have to be asleep at the wheel for them to drive the way they do. These are the ones who are usually driving in the lane just to the right of the slow lane. In other words, the ditch.

Rumor has it Picasso was a regular napper, painting most of his pieces right after waking up and before his eyes had focused. Napping made him an artistic legend.

Einstein napped, too, whenever he could (hence the bed hair). In fact, $E=MC^2$ came to him during a nap. He was actually dreaming about playing Scrabble and happened to write down some of the letters that he got stuck with. The 2 was just his lousy penmanship. But then someone mistook it for a scientific equation, and well, as they say, the rest is history.

All thanks to a nap.

Napoleon was also a napper. That's why he always had his hand in his jacket. He had his pillow tucked in there.

I knew an elderly man who used to fall asleep in church as soon as the pastor started preaching. He did it every Sunday, and he snored, too. He was a rather thin man. His wife was at least three times his size. So every Sunday she would wait for his head to drop, indicating that he had dozed off and was no longer aware of where he was. Then, with the first bear-like snore, she would rear back and give him a good jab with her ample arm, causing him to jump awake, startled and disoriented. One Sunday he called out in the middle of the sermon, "Stop it, woman! Can't you see I'm trying to sleep?!"

Ill-timed naps can get you into trouble. But again, the health benefits far outweigh any negative outcome (including bruising from a jab in the ribs). Medical research will back up the fact that napping can make you far more productive and alert. Some companies have even set up "nap rooms" to allow their employees the opportunity to recharge themselves. Some airports have opened "sleep centers," where you can get in a short nap between flights. These centers even have themed sleeping rooms, enabling nappers to fall asleep in the Caribbean, the Orient, or if they prefer, pure blackness. There are even nap rooms designed specifically for children.

This growing awareness of the benefits of napping is no doubt due to the round-the-clock activities that are thrust upon us today. Until a few decades ago, if you wanted to go shopping at three o'clock in the morning, you'd have a patrol car tailing you. Stores weren't open at that hour.

But now there are twenty-four-hour grocery stores and pharmacies, and you can shop online or from your couch while watching the Home Shopping Network on TV twenty-four hours a day. People don't sleep like they used to (if at all), and businesses are capitalizing on our fatigue.

So napping helps. According to a recent survey, napping is not only healthy, it burns up calories, too. Not a lot, but it does burn some. I'm not sure how it does this, but I assume if you snore, or better yet, toss and turn while you nap, this is what's burning up the calories.

If you walk in your sleep, you might even find yourself losing more weight (but always try to walk against traffic, and abide by all traffic signals).

My husband and I are polar opposites when it comes to napping. I rarely take a nap. He schedules one on his Day-Timer.

The following is a list of the variety of naps available to us. This list is by no means comprehensive, but it does provide a start.

The Middle-of-Your-Favorite-TV-Show Nap

This is the most common of all naps. It usually takes place in a recliner, but it has also been known to occur while the vulnerable person is stretched out on a sofa, draped over an ottoman, or lying prostrate on the floor in front of a television set. The identifying quality of this particular nap is what is known as "napper's denial." This can be witnessed the minute the television is turned off by a family member. The napper will immediately jump to his feet and declare, "Hey, what are you doing? I was watching that!"

The Cat Nap

Inspired by felines everywhere, the cat nap is a nap you take when your cat decides to fall asleep on your face. This isn't a very deep sleep because if you make the slightest noise or sudden movement, your cat will sink his claws into your eyebrows and you'll be forced to have him surgically removed. But it is still a popular nap, scratches and all.

The Middle-of-a-Sermon or After-Dinner-Speech Nap

This nap is by far the most noticeable nap because it usually takes place in an auditorium full of people. The number of people noticing the napper increases significantly, depending on at what point in the lecture or sermon the nap occurs. For example, if the napper dozes off during the song service, the nap can continue virtually unnoticed. (The main problem with song-service napping happens when the congregation is asked to stand. Without the other shoulders to lean on, the napper will slide down onto the pew and begin drooling on the upholstery.) However, if the nap occurs during the lecture or sermon, and the napper tends to talk in his or her sleep, an embarrassing verbal exchange could follow. Once awake, the napper rarely remembers these verbal exchanges and will need to buy an audiotape of the service to know what points he protested, and what ill-timed "Amen"s he has to take back.

The After-Lunch Nap

This nap hits after eating lunch—hence the name. No matter how hard you try to keep your eyes open after a hearty meal, they will slam shut after that last bite like an automatic door over which you have no control. It really doesn't matter what you ate for lunch. You could have eaten at an all-you-can-eat buffet, or perhaps you just had a salad. Either way, you'll find yourself dozing off before you even get to the dessert. And that, my friends, would be a tragedy.

The Thanksgiving-Feast Nap

The Thanksgiving-Feast Nap has also been referred to as "the nap of least resistance." It really shouldn't even be listed here because in most instances it would qualify for a coma, not a nap.

Millions of Americans succumb to this particular nap the fourth Thursday of every November. This unconscious state has been widely blamed on an ingredient found in turkey meat called *tryptophan*. Apparently, tryptophan is an amino acid that works like a natural sedative, leaving you with the uncontrollable desire to sleep. (It could also have something to do with the quart of gravy nestled atop that mountain of mashed potatoes, accompanied by three scoops of green bean casserole, two cups of yams, eight rolls, and four slices of pecan pie. But it's probably the tryptophan.)

The Driving Nap

It's not so much that a person can't nap and drive at the same time. Of course they can. I've personally seen plenty of drivers doing this. But it's a matter of *where* you do the sleeping. Napping while parked at red lights and Stop signs seems to be perfectly okay. You don't even have to worry about oversleeping, because the horn on the car behind you will serve as the ideal alarm clock. And the horn on the car behind *that* car will make a perfect snooze alarm a few light changes later.

For the driving napper looking for longer siestas, there are other ways that won't affect your fellow motorists. My favorite is the "car transport truck" nap. For this nap, you'll need to find an empty car transport truck parked at a red light. Once you do, try to catch the driver while he's listening to his radio and not paying attention. As soon as he's properly distracted, maneuver your car onto the ramp of the transport truck. Once you've driven your car onboard and it's securely in place, shift to Park and nap all the way to Tallahassee!

The Grandkids-Just-Got-Picked-Up Nap

This nap is induced by the sight of the rear taillights of your daughter's car as she drives away with the grandkids after an enjoyable but exhausting visit. Almost hypnotic in its pull, the grandkids-just-got-picked-up nap is one of the most addictive kinds of naps. Whenever you watch the grandkids, you will no doubt crave this nap.

The Dentist-Chair Nap

As impossible as this seems, the dentist-chair nap really does exist. Even though you just passed an anxiety-filled hour sitting in the waiting room, once the Novocain sets in, what else can you do but fall asleep, drilling noises and all?

The Hair-and-Nail-Salon Nap

Sure, your hairstylist, barber, or nail designer may enjoy talking to you while you're being primped and worked on, but experienced nappers know that this is the prime location and opportunity for the ultimate nap. There is something about having your hair shampooed and brushed, or your hands and fingers massaged, that beats every lullaby known to man.

The Twenty-Winks Nap

This is no wives' tale. This nap really does exist. Granted, there are cases on record where a twenty-winks nap was mistaken for a tic, but regardless, this still remains one of the most popular naps today.

There you have it. This is just a small sampling of the many kinds of naps that are available to nappers today. So don't just sit there trying your hardest to keep your eyelids pried open. Go ahead and close them! Take a nap! Recharge those batteries! Rest your eyes and improve your focus! And…

and…

and…

Zzzzzzzzz…

Breaking News

Remember the good ol' days when a breaking news alert was something worthy of interrupting your regular programming? Because the news item was so important, you understood why the network had to break in to your show. Perhaps war had broken out or peace had been declared or the president had been shot at by an assassin's bullet. Whatever it was, you knew it had to be an important news bulletin for the network to cut in to your soap opera. Back then, no network would have been brave enough to try doing that without good reason.

But all of that has changed now. These days *everything* is a breaking news item. Why, there can be four or five breaking news items in one day. Sometimes in one hour. Many of these "news alerts" don't qualify as an emergency in the least. The networks have simply discovered that the "breaking news flash" is a good way to get our attention and make us stay tuned.

Comparing the news alerts of yesterday to the news alerts of today would look something like this:

YESTERDAY'S BREAKING NEWS	TODAY'S BREAKING NEWS
"Man lands on the moon!"	"Britney Spears loses custody battle!"
"Bobby Kennedy shot!"	"*My Name Is Earl* gets renewed!"
"Watergate break-in exposed!"	"Jennifer Aniston discovers new mole."
"Cuban Missile Crisis escalates!"	"Angelina and Brad attempt to adopt Madonna's adopted baby."
"Wall Street crashes!"	"Seasons change. Leaves turn. Stay tuned!"
"Gas shortage causes price hike."	"*Nothing* causes gas price hike . . . again!"
"Southern California fires— film at eleven."	"SpongeBob preempts State of the Union Address!"
"Inflation and unemployment hits all-time high."	"Paris Hilton doesn't appear on a single magazine cover this month!"
"Cold War intensifies."	"Tom Cruise takes back everything he's ever said."
"Hostages released!"	"Oscar telecast has no political statements for captive worldwide audience. Can the end of the world be far behind?"

I'm not sure how we return to a less-hysterical society, but it sure would be nice, wouldn't it? What's happening is we're getting so numb to these "New Alerts" and "Breaking News" stories that when something serious really happens, we're going to continue going about our day and not pay much attention. We won't evacuate when a hurricane is about to hit. We won't duck when a meteor is hurling toward earth. We won't realize that Wall Street has just crashed, and we'll go ahead and invest our life savings in it. We're crying "Wolf!" over every little thing, but there are a lot of real wolves out there that we need to be informed about. So let's go back to saving the news alerts for real news. As for all the other non-news items, reporters should let us find out that kind of news the way people always used to . . . gossiping over the backyard fence.

Enjoying the Peace and Quiet

After enduring the parenting years filled with teenage sleepovers, garage band practices, sibling bickering, and endless teenage phone conversations, you would think you would be able to look forward to a little peace and quiet in your later years. Unfortunately, it doesn't work that way.

Life is noisy. If you haven't noticed that simple fact, open your windows and take a listen. From booming car radios to garbage trucks to sirens and car alarms going off at all hours of the night, to overhead aircraft sounding like they're conducting war games above your house, where can you find any peace and quiet these days?

You can't even watch television without being startled out of your wits every time a high-decibel commercial comes on. Why do networks and cable stations keep doing this to us? Do they own stock in defibrillation machines? You'll be right in the middle of watching *Howard's End* or *Out of Africa*, and then, all of a sudden, a car dealer or product salesman will burst onto the screen, hocking his wares at a noise level that's akin to Amtrak pulling into your living room. Are they trying to get rid of us baby boomers all at once so the MTV generation can once and for all rule the airwaves? I'm not accusing anyone. I'm just bringing up the possible motives.

I believe that may be the best thing to look forward to about our retirement years—some of the noises we'll no longer have to hear. Like the alarm clock. Is there any noise more irritating than an alarm clock? Whether it buzzes or rings or plays happy tunes or crows like a rooster, it's still an unwelcome intrusion.

But once we've retired, the alarm clock is one noise we can happily check off our list.

Another noise we will no longer have to put up with, or at least not as much, is our cell phone or pager. Of course, we'll still receive calls from family and friends, but our boss's calls should taper off after retirement. Unless our filing system was so bad no one can find anything after we leave.

We won't hear as many car horns after we retire, either. Car horns are the concerto of the working class. Whether you hit the early morning traffic jam, the midmorning traffic jam, the early afternoon traffic jam, or the five-o'clock rush, you've no doubt had your fill of honking horns. Thankfully, after retirement, car-horn concerts are a far less common occurrence.

In their place will be new, different sounds that you didn't used to hear, or at least didn't hear as clearly, when you were working. Sounds like your grandchildren asking you to toss a football around in the yard. Or the sound of the motor purring in that RV that's been sitting idle in your driveway for the past five years. And the best sound yet—the sound of the tree branches blowing above you in the wind as you lay stretched out on your hammock—the one you hung twelve summers ago but have laid in only twice. Those sounds. That's what you'll hear.

And that can be a concert to beat all concerts.

Ten Advantages to Global Warming (For the Middle-Aged Person)

1. No more fighting with your spouse over the blankets.
2. Global warming increases the potency of your deep-heating ointment.
3. You no longer have to bring a jacket on your annual Alaskan cruise.
4. Fewer trees to dodge on your driver's license test.
5. The bubbling asphalt improves the circulation in your feet.
6. No more going through hot flashes alone. Night sweats are now a family activity.
7. Due to excessive heat, swimming in wishing wells is now legal. So instead of paying for a gym membership that you never use, you're making money with every lap you swim.
8. Elevated water temperatures will pre-cook fish.
9. Because of increased flooding, our gas-guzzling cars will be cheaper to operate when we've turned them into rowboats.
10. Seniors and middle-aged people will no longer be the only age groups with sun spots.

Ten Stupid Things Middle-Aged Women Do to Mess Up Their Lives

1. Volunteer to watch all five grandchildren on the first day of their chicken pox outbreak.

2. Hit four consecutive outlet malls without remembering at which one she left her husband.

3. Ride the triple-upside-down roller coaster with granddaughter. Twice. After eating two orders of jalapeño nachos.

4. Sit cross-legged on the floor for longer than seven seconds.

5. Fail to put a lock on the thermostat during menopause.

6. Wear a turtleneck.

7. Put car keys and glasses anywhere but around the neck . . . with Post-it Note on forehead reminding her of their whereabouts.

8. Forget where she put her ginseng.

9. Attempt to break the limbo record at thirtieth high school reunion.

10. Try putting on control-top anything without the Jaws of Life on standby.

Second-Childhood Board Games

When I was growing up, my siblings and I loved to play board games. To make it more challenging, we'd usually play with a few side rules—like the loser would have to wash a pile of dishes, dust the furniture, or do a load of laundry. This took some of the pain out of housekeeping and gave a little added incentive to winning.

Most of us boomers have fond memories of playing board games in our childhood, and some of us still enjoy them today. So aside from Bingo, why aren't game-manufacturing companies capitalizing on this wide-open market?

Good question, huh?

I would, therefore, like to take this opportunity to propose the following boomer game ideas to Mattel, Hasbro, and any other board-game company who might be reading this:

Battle (Cruise) Ship

Similar to the popular Battleship game, except with this version your strategy is to sink all the game pieces of other hungry seniors, so you can move in and claim your victory at the front of the buffet line.

Cramps and Bladders

Much like the ever-popular children's game Chutes and Ladders, only the goal of this game is to get around the board without a single leg cramp or incontinence problem. It's harder than it sounds (especially if you're sitting cross-legged on the floor, or if you just had three glasses of sweet tea).

Middle-Age-onopoly

This is based on the popular Monopoly game, only instead of the familiar properties, the journey around the board takes you through the Middle-Aged years. You might land on properties such as *Sitting in the* Park Place, Reading *Glasses* Railroad, New *Knee* Avenue, and the ever-dreaded *Go to the Home! Go Directly to the Home. Do Not Pass Go and Do Not Collect $200!* card.

Ribbage

A lot like the popular game of Cribbage, except the only goal of this game is to roll the dice while simultaneously reaching across the table to get your snacks without cracking a single rib.

Don't Have a Clue

Similar to the game of Clue, this game also has players moving their game pieces between the library, the dining room, and all the other rooms on the board. But once inside, they can't remember why they went into that room in the first place.

Strained Back-Gammon

Similar to the age-old game of backgammon, the goal of this game is to move your checkers around the board without pulling your back out.

Twister ER

Speaking of pulling your back out, this game works on the same principle as the regular game of Twister, only with middle-aged players there tends to be more emergency room services needed.

Irritation

Like the popular board game Aggravation, players try to make it "home" without losing any of their marbles.

The Game of Middle-Aged Life

Comparable to the original Game of Life, this version is specifically geared for the over-fifty crowd. Instead of picking up new children as you drive along the board, you pick up college kids returning home or carjackers trying to steal your automobile (at least in the Los Angeles version).

Disconnect Four

Remember playing Connect Four with your children? Well, now you can play it once again, only this version is Disconnect Four. Object of the game? Be the first player to get four of your checkers in a row before disconnecting your shoulder from reaching across the table to the bowl of popcorn.

Vertigo

This is the middle-aged version of Stratego. The object of the game is to capture your opponent's flag without passing out on the board from too much spicy salsa and bean dip.

Babble

Similar to the popular game of Scrabble, except the words cannot be challenged. Imagine being able to claim points for such words as "muffritch" and "xigilch." The points would be limitless.

Chinese Checkers and Takeout

Exactly like the old Chinese Checkers game, only this one comes with takeout. If you're going to play a game, you might as well eat while you're doing it. With four players, you add egg rolls. The downside? An hour later, you're ready to play again.

A "Wait" Problem

According to those who research these sorts of things, the average wait in an emergency room today is one hour. That may sound like a long time, but it's not that bad, really, considering how much there is to do to kill time in a hospital waiting room. For example, you can:

- Watch medical dramas on television and learn how to perform your own surgery or defibrillation, just in case you need to go ahead and take action yourself.
- Catch up on all those magazine articles you missed four years ago.
- Try to figure out what's wrong with everyone else in the room . . . and exactly how far away from them you should sit.
- Get in touch with all your old friends as you call to tell them you're in the emergency room. In an hour's time, you can get pretty far down the alphabet.
- Buy a bag of pretzels in their vending machine so in case you should choke on one, you'll be in the right place . . . provided you can wait out the hour for a Heimlich.

- If you're mobile, you can walk the halls of the hospital and wave to all the patients. Do not, however, offer them medical advice . . . unless it was something you just saw on *ER* and it had a happy ending. (NOTE: If the patient's regular doctor is there, I wouldn't interrupt.)
- Spell-check all the wall posters. A typo on a medical poster can be serious. There is a big difference between "apply pressure to stop the bleeding" and "apply pressure to stop the bleating."
- Get your exercise by repeatedly moving away from the wrestling six-year-olds who keep tumbling into you.
- Pour yourself a cup of the free coffee. You might need it later to touch up the paint on your car should it get sideswiped in the parking lot.
- Count the number of times the automatic doors open and close. Multiply that figure by how many times you've heard the announcement about keeping the driveway clear for ambulances. Then subtract your age and add the number of dark-haired people in the waiting room. Why? Who cares? You've got an hour to kill!

This story originally appeared on New Christian Voices, *www.newchristianvoices.com/column/marthas-laugh-lines-a-wait-problem*, August 8, 2008.

Discover the Power of Your Regrets and Whining

What Were We Thinking?

Remember those hippie names of the '70s? Many of us were naming our kids (or renaming ourselves) calm, peaceful names like:

Moonflower
Sun-dancer
Sky-bird
Starlight
Summer Breeze
Rainbow Raine
Zoey Wind
Echo
Spirit
Mist
Moon Java

Can you picture these kids (or us) at a retirement home someday? The facility newsletter would sound something like this:

We're sorry to report that Sun-dancer, who turns eighty today, fell last night and ripped a ligament in his knee. We also have good news to share—Starlight got her new Hover-craft delivered today. All the seventy-year-old could say was, "Groovy!" Moonflower and Moon Java are forming a protest march against the nursing home staff at noon. Meet in the cafeteria by eleven-thirty and bring your love beads and your parent permission slip to give to Sky-bird. (Just kidding about the parent permission slip. A little nursing home humor.)

It makes you wonder what we were thinking back then, doesn't it? A name is something that sticks with us through all phases of our lives. What sounds cool to us in our twenties might not sound so "groovy" to us in our eighties.

Then again, maybe it'll make life in the home a lot more interesting. That's coming from a lady who once thought about changing her name to Thyme, but I could never remember how to spell it. So what do I know?

What Chocolate Dreams May Come

I knew if I just lived long enough, my dreams would come true. And they have. Have you heard about this? There is a new line of "chocolate" beauty products. Yes, you read that right. A new line of *chocolate* beauty products!

Here are just some of the products that are offered: chocolate cherry instant facial; chocolate cherry pedicure cream that exfoliates, softens, and moisturizes the skin; chocolate body spray; and even chocolate soap. In fact, just about any toiletry item you want is now available in chocolate. *This is wonderful news!* Why wasn't the day these products first hit the market declared a national holiday? What's up with that, Washington?

Chocolate beauty products are just the thing that will hold most of us over until someone comes out with a twenty-four-hour chocolate patch.

Imagine it—now, instead of getting mad when you accidentally bite your bottom lip, you'll taste your chocolate lipstick and just keep chewing on it for a while.

Chocolate facial creams would come in handy if you're ever stuck out in the wilderness. You could conceivably have enough chocolate tucked away in your pores to tide you over until help comes. Of course, the downside to this is that the scent could also attract bears. But even that's a small price to pay for transportable facial chocolate.

The only product I don't understand, though, is the chocolate pedicure. What good does it do us to have feet that smell like chocolate? It's not like we go around smelling our feet all day. (If you do, you need another hobby.)

I can, however, fully understand the chocolate shampoo. All we'd have to do is grab a handful of our hair and smell it whenever we're hungry or bored. Some of us might even stick a few strands in our mouth and suck on it from time to time. (If you've lost all your hair, don't feel discouraged. You can use the chocolate soap on your scalp. Or look into getting a Tootsie Roll transplant.)

Chocolate beauty products—who would have ever thought we'd live long enough to see this. Like Yakov Smirnoff would say: What a country!

Ten Things a Menopausal Woman Should Never Do

1. Allow her husband to buy an electric blanket.
2. Sign up for assertiveness training.
3. Go to a sauna.
4. Load the gun.
5. Vacation in Florida in mid-July.
6. Move to the back of an overcrowded elevator.
7. Try to put on Spanx right out of the shower.
8. Close the lid on a tanning bed.
9. Run out of Kleenex.
10. Wear leather pants.

Women and Politics

"All I am or can be, I owe to my angel mother."
Abraham Lincoln

This generation has seen more and more women entering the political arena. But if we think the fairer sex is just beginning to have influence over how our country is run, we'd be sorely mistaken. Women have been influencing political decisions ever since our nation began. How, you ask, when they couldn't even vote back then?

The influence came through their mothering.

When Joe Biden introduced his mother at a recent political rally, it was easy to see how he became the man that he is. Joe's mom is one great lady!

With the camera fixed on Catherine Eugenia Finnegan Biden, then-Senator Biden began to extol the motherly virtues of this beautiful woman. He told us how she had taught him that "failure at some point in everyone's life is inevitable, but giving up is unforgivable."

He also told how, in his younger years, he used to have a stuttering problem. But his mom lovingly explained to him that "it was because I was so bright I couldn't get the thoughts out quickly enough." He also said that "when I was not as well dressed as others, she told me how handsome she thought I was. When I got knocked down by guys bigger than me, she sent me back out and demanded that I bloody their noses so I could walk down that street the next day."

Catherine Biden blushed and sheepishly nodded when he quoted that last instruction.

After the tragic car accident some years ago that took the life of Joe Biden's first wife and his infant daughter on their way home from picking out their Christmas tree, his mother told him, "Joey, God sends no cross you cannot bear."

That is one great mother.

To be fair, Barbara Bush is another great mom. She has a lot of wisdom and heart, too. Barbara once said, "If human beings are perceived as potentials rather than problems, as possessing strengths instead of weaknesses, as unlimited rather than dull and unresponsive, then they thrive and grow to their capabilities."

Like Joe Biden, Barbara and George Bush Sr. also had tragedy strike their lives. They lost a four-year-old daughter to leukemia. That loss was, I'm sure, the foundation for this belief of Barbara's: "You have to love your children unselfishly. That is hard. But it is the only way."

The loss of a child, or a spouse, as difficult as that is to go through, gives one depth. So does helping your son or daughter overcome a physical or other kind of life challenge. It will drive you to your knees. And on your knees is a good place to be, especially for someone in the position of leading our country. Barbara was right when she said, "You may think the president is all-powerful, but he is not. He needs a lot of guidance from the Lord."

President Lincoln was greatly influenced by his stepmother, and President Bill Clinton often shared how his mother's sacrifices and unconditional love had a positive effect on his life.

So the next time an election year rolls around, maybe we shouldn't fret so much over the debates, the political ads, and all those campaign promises. In fact, maybe it's time we gave up the notion of a president altogether. Maybe what's needed is a national "Mom."

The Housing Slump

Since the housing market hasn't fully recovered from its slump yet, home designers are incorporating all sorts of new ideas into their housing plans to coax buyers to come out and see their product.

One of the hottest new concepts to come along is the snoring room. This room is just off of the master bedroom, and it is for the one who has to listen to the snoring; it's not for the snorer. This saves the non-snorer from having to sleep on the sofa, which is often too far away, or having to do the pillow sandwich method of snore control (one pillow over each ear). The snoring room helps the non-snorer escape discreetly to a quieter area, somewhere where the walls aren't buckling from the noise.

Some of these snoring rooms even come with a bath. I guess that's in case you need to add running water to aid in the noise reduction. (That's why so many people vacation at Niagara Falls, you know. It isn't for the view. It's because all that water cascading over the cliff is the only thing that'll drown out their spouse's snoring.)

Another good idea is the gift-wrapping room. This is a small room, about the size of a laundry room, where all you do is wrap presents. I love to give gifts, so this would be a dream room for me. And with a lock, it would be the perfect place to hide Christmas toys, too.

Some model homes have doggie showers. That's a great idea. Why not let your dog enjoy warm water just like you get to every day, or rather just like you *would* get to if the person before you didn't always beat you to the hot water.

One more new concept is the rejuvenation room or personal spa. Who among us doesn't need a little space to relax and get ready to face the world again? These rooms are more than a workout room. They're like a private mini day spa. You can spend twenty minutes in there, an hour, or the rest of the day. In fact, you may not ever want to leave that room again.

My favorite concept is heated patios or a patio with a built-in fireplace. How nice is that? You could enjoy a roaring fire on your patio and it wouldn't have anything to do with a fireworks show gone bad.

Heated bathroom and kitchen floors are now offered in some home designs. No more getting up in the middle of the night and getting frostbite when you walk into the bathroom or go to get yourself a glass of water.

Even with all these great designs, they're still missing a few good ones. For instance, wouldn't you love to see a Post-it Note room? This would be a special room where you could stick up all those wonderful little memos to yourself and other family members. It wouldn't need to be a big room, either. Post-it Notes are small. It would just need to provide a lot of empty wall space.

With a Post-it Note room, whenever you wanted to know what you're supposed to be doing, what time you were supposed to be doing it, or even why you walked into the room in the

first place, all you'd have to do is look around until you found the appropriate sticky note.

Housing designs can always be improved upon, and it's nice to know that builders are offering us so many new and unique plans to choose from. But no matter how many rooms a house may have, it still only needs one thing to make it a home—love. And that can't be put into the design. It has to walk through the doors with you every morning and night.

They Don't Write Them Like They Used To

One night while my husband was working at one of the Los Angeles police department's precincts, a group of officers working the phone lines started talking about their favorite old television shows. The subject came around to *Sheriff John*, a local children's show watched religiously by many of the officers in their childhood. It didn't take long before one of the officers broke into song.

"Put another candle on my birthday cake. My birthday cake . . . My birthday Caaaaa-ake. Put another candle on my birthday cake. I'm another year old today."

(If you remember *Sheriff John*, then you know the tune.)

The officer had fully intended to only sing a few bars of the song, but after the other officers joined in, they ended up singing the whole song. Several times.

The Sheriff John Happy Birthday Song may never have won a Grammy, but that song and its words are so much a part of our generation, at least in the L.A. area, that some forty plus years later most of us can still recite it from memory.

I'm sure we could all sing along with *Mr. Ed*'s theme song, too, or the theme songs to *Leave It to Beaver*, *Gilligan's Island*, *The Munsters*, or *Green Acres*.

We could hum the *Lone Ranger*'s theme song, *I Love Lucy*'s, or the theme songs from *The Honeymooners* or *The Dick Van Dyke Show*.

We could whistle along to the theme of *The Andy Griffith Show* or snap our fingers to the theme song from *The Addams Family*.

Go on, try it right now. Belt one of them out. Don't worry, Simon Cowell's not going to hear it. Take yourself back to the '50s and '60s, and maybe even the '70s. Relive your youth. If you're at Starbucks or on a plane reading this, and someone looks at you funny, pay them no mind. After all, haven't you been putting up with their whiny kid and incessant cell phone calls all morning? Now it's your turn!

So all together now . . .

"A horse is a horse, of course, of course . . ."

The New/Old Fall Season

Hollywood is constantly on the lookout for the next television hit, but they've already got it. All they have to do is look on their shelves and dust off a few masterpieces, throw in some political correctness, add some edge, update them a little, and voila! . . . a winning pilot season!

So what are they waiting for? A nudge from us boomers? Well, they can now consider themselves duly nudged. So if they take the bait, here are a few of the shows we might soon be seeing:

The Lone Ranger—Special Crimes Unit

With Tonto, his trusty friend of Native American descent by his side, the Lone Ranger always seems to show up at just the right time. But what exactly does "Hi-yo Silver, Away!" mean, anyway? The word *Silver* could be some kind of discriminatory slur against the elderly. Tune in to find out as the Civil Liberties Union asks, "Who was that masked man?"

Desperate Bozos

Bozo, a clown of renown, lives in a neighborhood where life is a circus. He has to deal with life, work, and his neighbors, most of which are a bunch of clowns.

Mayberry 90210

This town is a mix between Mayberry and Beverly Hills. It's the same beloved characters—Andy and Barney and Betty Lou and Aunt Bea—but these actors have all had extensive plastic surgery and drive Hummers around Mayberry.

I Love Dr. Phil

Dr. Phil Ricardo, family therapist and bongo player, helps his guests learn to face their issues while, at the same time, doing his best to keep his wife, Lucy, out of show business.

Dancing With the Dummies

Ballroom dancing competition with former stars of the dummy persuasion. Howdy Doody, Charlie McCarthy, Jerry Mahoney, and others compete to see who will take home the coveted prize—to be a real boy like Pinocchio.

I Dream of Seinfeld

A show about nothing, starring a genie who never leaves her bottle and doesn't grant anyone any wishes. Especially the Soup Nazi.

CSI: Green Acres

CSI agents get assigned to the farm community of Green Acres to investigate cattle rustling.

Are You Smarter Than Fonzie?

Contestants try to stump the Fonz by answering more questions correctly than he can. "Aaay!"

Laverne and O'Reilley

Laverne shows news commentator Bill O'Reilley an unconventional look at today's headlines. "One, two, three, four, five, six, seven, eight. Schlemiel! Schlimazel! No Spin Zone incorporated!"

Ozzie's Anatomy

Ozzie, with Harriet's full backing, has gone to medical school and is now practicing at a hospital in Seattle. But he flies home every night in time to be with his family for dinner.

Times Change

It's funny how times change. Whenever I look back over my high school yearbooks or through family albums, I'm always amazed at the difference between then and now. Not that either one was better. They're just different. Let me show you what I mean:

THAT WAS THEN	THIS IS NOW
Can't go anywhere because you have no wheels	Can't go anywhere because you forgot where you've parked your wheels
Can't wait to start a savings account for retirement	Can't wait to start a savings account for retirement
"Turn up the radio!"	"Turn up the radio!"
It's 10:00. Do you know where your children are?	It's 7:00. Do you know where your bed is?
Keeping a diary	Keeping a medication log
Slumber parties where you stay up all night	Nights of insomnia where you stay up all night
Growing pains	Restless leg syndrome

Hitting all the hot spots	Counting all the age spots
Cruising the boulevard	Cruising the open sea
Hoping that cute football player will call you and make a date	Hope your podiatrist will call and schedule an appointment

Oh well, you know what they say—as the times change, we have to change with them—at least as much as we feel comfortable doing. It's a simple matter of survival of the flexible.

Best Friends of Young and Old Alike

Pets are wonderful companions for any age group. But for those of us approaching retirement age, pets are not only helpful and a good source of unconditional love, they're healthy for us, too.

Let's talk about unconditional love first. Dogs don't care if your face has pillow creases, how bad your breath is (theirs is usually worse), or whether your hair is sticking straight up in the air or is minding its own business on the nightstand. They love you anyway. They will dance around in circles just because you walk into the room. They'll jump up and lick your face simply because you exist. They will sit and stare out the window and watch you drive away for as long as they can see you. And they might even continue whimpering until you return home. Dogs will sit and listen to you for as long as you want to talk. They'll wag their tails even when you don't feel like wagging yours. And should anything happen to you, they'll mourn a lot longer than at the funeral. No wonder dogs are called "man's best friend."

Their unconditional acceptance is good for our psyche. They don't care if we're overdue on our electric bill, if our dishes aren't done, or if we're three weeks behind on answering our e-mail. They love and accept us for who we are—the good, the bad, and the procrastinating.

Since dogs, in particular, and pets, in general, are so healthy for us, don't you wish we had a better way to communicate with them?

Well, wish no more. There is a product on the market right now that helps us interpret certain pet sounds. It's similar to what they have for moms and dads to figure out what their infant is trying to tell them when they wake up crying every hour. Do they want a bottle? Do they need changing? Do they want to catch up on the overseas stock report?

Well, the same technology is available for pets. You simply attach the mechanism to the dog's collar, and when the dog barks, it will document its voiceprint, which is then transmitted to a receiver that displays up to two hundred phrases that the dog might be saying, such as:

"I'm hungry."

"I'm thirsty."

"You're not the boss of me!"

Or *"The cat's going down!"*

The owner will enter the correct request for that voiceprint into the machine. So the next time the dog barks, the machine will match that voiceprint, and the corresponding request will display on the receiver.

Gone are the days of wondering what your dog is barking at. If it's a stray animal in the yard, the machine will tell you. If he simply wants you to turn off the evening news and pay him some attention, the machine will tell you. If he's hungry and not interested in the dried-out morsels of pet food you've been giving him, the machine will tell you. If nothing's bothering him but he just wants to tick off the neighbors, the machine will tell you.

Imagine how much easier this is going to make our lives.

Let's even go one step further. What if they made one of these machines to interpret the all-too-familiar husband "grunt." Most grunts sound alike, so it's difficult to know what a husband is saying when you hear one of them.

But if there were a machine that would interpret these grunts, life would be so much easier on all of us. With a simple click, we'd be able to know whether the grunt means:

"Where's dinner?"

"Keep your hands off my popcorn."

"Move over; you're blocking my view of the Super Bowl."

"Happy anniversary, dear."

"Hey, I think you've lost some weight."

"What do you mean, I never communicate? This is communicating!"

See, I knew if we just hung around long enough, life—and marriage—would get easier.

Duly Warned

I recently discovered a great new little gadget. It's a sensor that you can install on your car that will indicate when you're getting too close to hitting something—like a shopping cart, another car, a pedestrian, or the side of a church (yes, I did hit one once).

This new device is called the Park Zone, and it's for those of us who tend to take out a hot-water heater and half a living room when pulling into our garages. Age really has nothing to do with it. I believe the same middle-aged people who are running over a row of trash cans as they drive out of their cul-de-sac are the same ones who were running over a row of trash cans when they were driving away from their college dorm.

Regardless, I think the Park Zone is a great idea. Imagine it—three-car parallel-parking pileups could be a thing of the past. No more, "Whoops! I guess that's close enough." Or "My bad. I thought I had more room than that."

This "zone indicator" technology can help us in many other areas of our lives, too. Like, maybe they could come out with a Shopping Cart Zone. Runaway shopping carts can be hazardous to the paint job on cars. But if we had shopping cart zone indicators, we could know exactly how close a runaway cart was getting to our vehicle and go chasing after it before any real damage could be done.

A Stroller Zone would be a welcome device, too. Wouldn't you like to hear a buzzer sound whenever a mother, pushing her child's stroller, comes dangerously close to the first layer of your ankle skin?

A Fan Zone would come in handy at sporting events. Before someone sits down in the seat next to you, a Fan Zone could warn him, even in the midst of his exuberance, that he's about to knock over your overpriced cup of soda.

People should have zone indicators, too. These would especially come in handy with "close talkers." There's nothing worse than getting stuck standing next to a close talker. A People Zone would let the close talker know when they're moving into your space. I don't know about you, but I prefer only my dentist looking that closely at my dental work.

Zone indicators would be good for air travel, as well. Then if the person next to you dozes off and nods onto your shoulder, the alarm would sound to wake him or her up before the drooling begins.

I suppose until someone with an entrepreneurial gifting comes along and manufactures a few of these wonder products, we'll have to continue making our way through life dealing with these matters ourselves. But at least for now, we've got the Park Zone for our cars. So the parallel parking portion of our next driving exams should start getting easier.

And as long as there aren't any church buildings that I have to maneuver my way around, I should ace mine!

Hurry Up!

It's amazing how impatient we've become these days. I remember when microwaves first came out. We couldn't believe that an oven could cook an entire potato in less than ten minutes.

Now we stand next to the microwave and tap our fingers impatiently if anything takes longer than ninety seconds to nuke to perfection.

When the concept of fast food was first introduced, we were amazed to realize that all we had to do was order into a microphone and then drive around the building to pick up our food.

Now if it's not ready when we speed around the corner, we're ticked off. And if we're told we'll have to pull up past the window and wait for our order to be brought out to us, we're ready to talk to the manager. Or someone's momma.

The computer isn't even fast enough for us anymore. Notice your reaction the next time your PC or Mac freezes up on you for ten seconds. That will be the longest ten seconds of your life.

And waiting for your MapQuest directions to be printed out seems like an eternity. Doesn't your printer know you've got to get going? *You don't have the three seconds to spare for this!*

Remember when we had to wait the entire weekend to do our banking? Now we can't even wait on a Saturday afternoon while the ATM machine goes through its prompts. *English or Spanish? Come on already! I'm late for work!*

Once, while trying to get some money out of an ATM machine, I pressed the *Spanish* button by mistake. But since I was in a hurry, I figured I'd go ahead and finish the transaction that way. After all, I went all the way to Spanish 6 in high school.

I had to press Cancel at about the third prompt. Or make that *Numero Whatever It Was.*

No one has time to wait anymore. We want our instant oatmeal, minute rice, one-hour photo, and thirty-day weight-loss program *NOW!*

We want to learn to play the guitar in seven days and earn a college degree in mere weeks (or as long as it takes for the Internet auction site to mail it to us).

We can't wait for our kids or grandkids to grow up, Christmas to get here, the Super Bowl to be played, and our .00001% interest on our savings account of $4.98 to kick in and make us rich.

We can't even let our grass grow on its own anymore. We have to hurry it along with all sorts of growth stimulants. Even our fruits and vegetables are being picked early from the farm and forced to ripen on their way to the grocery store. Some farm animals are given medications to speed along their growth, too.

What's wrong with us? Where are we all rushing to? Have we forgotten what it means to rest? To slow down and look at the scenery along the way? To enjoy each stage of life? To pick fruit from a tree at the peak of its ripeness? To actually cook a meal the old-fashioned way, with real pots and pans and steam (or black smoke, as the case may be).

Each one of us has been allotted only a certain amount of time here on this earth. Why are we trying our hardest to get to the end so quickly?

It's time to slow down, take a deep breath, and enjoy our lives. And leave the speeding for the racetrack.

This story originally appeared on New Christian Voices, *www.newchristianvoices.com/column/marthas-laugh-lines-whats-hurry*, August 21, 2008.

Retirement Pros and Cons

Those who know about these sorts of things say that whenever you're faced with making an important decision, it is a good idea to make a list of the pros and cons of your choices. This helps you to see which side of the equation has the most benefits.

One of the most difficult decisions any of us will ever have to make is whether to retire or to keep on working. If you are currently faced with such a decision, here is a list of the possible benefits for each side to help you figure out which is the right path for you.

Continuing to Work	**Retirement**
Your boss complains about your midday nap.	Your spouse complains about your midday nap.
You wonder if you've saved enough for retirement.	You know you didn't save enough for retirement.
You have the energy to mow your lawn, but no time.	You have the time to mow your lawn, but no energy.

You know the names of everyone at your company and they feel like family.

You know the names of everyone on The Weather Channel and they feel like family.

You have plenty of money, but no time to go where you want to.

You have plenty of time, but no money to go where you want to go.

You count down the days on your calendar until retirement.

You've lost track of what day it is, and you can't find your calendar.

You put AARP mailings aside to read someday.

You put AARP mailings aside to read someday.

Living above your means.

You have no means.

You wish the old codger driving in front would speed up.

You wish the jerk riding your tail would slow down.

It's 7:00 A.M. Time to wake up.

It's 7:00 P.M. Time to go to bed.

Let Go of the Pork Chop

The Over-Fifty Diet Plan

"I am not a glutton. I am an explorer of food."
Erma Bombeck

Diets come and go. Much of what they told us not to eat yesterday is perfectly fine to eat today, and in some cases even recommended. How do they expect us to keep up?

Celebrity diet plans are the ones that seem to gain the most momentum and spread across the country like wildfire. It doesn't matter if the celebrity has actually lost any weight on their diet, or if they have gained it all back since posing for their "after" picture—we still want to follow their diet plan.

But where's a diet plan specifically for those of us over fifty? Don't we need one especially tailored to our needs? Of course we do! Just as we have our own special vitamins, our own conventions, and our own menu items, those of us over fifty need our own diet plan, too.

So here's an Over-Fifty Diet Plan that might help you lose weight, but regardless, you'll be a lot happier through the process. Here's how it works:

- First, eat white bread only if it's in the form of bread pudding. The cinnamon in the pudding cancels out any negative effects of the white flour, and the raisins are an excellent source of iron.

- Avoid animal fat. It is bad. Animal cookies, on the other hand, are fine. If you sandwich a vitamin between them, they're even healthy. So distract the grandkids' attention and grab yourself a few. Or a handful. Oh, all right, go ahead and grab whatever you can take without the child pitching a fit and blowing your cover. If you can, try to get all the elephants. They tend to be bigger and can cover the larger multivitamins.

- Weight resistance is an important part of some celebrity diet plans. It is an important part of this Over-Fifty Diet Plan, too. Daily bench press twenty pounds of pound cake (roughly twenty cakes), reducing the pounds of cake by five-pound increments as you cool down. How you choose to reduce the pound cake is up to you; however, eating it does seem to be the most efficient.

- Most people don't get enough vegetables, fruits, and nuts in their daily diet. Because of this, the Over-Fifty Diet Plan recommends doubling the amount of shredded carrots, pineapple, and walnuts in your carrot cake.

- Use only 100 percent virgin olive oil to deep-fry your Twinkies.

- Much like the three-hour diet (which recommends timing your food intake to approximately every three hours), the Over-Fifty Diet Plan recommends timing your meals, too. But instead of a clock, this diet recommends using a three-minute egg timer. You don't have to eat much, but every three minutes you should be eating something. How can this possibly help you lose weight, you ask? Why, the sheer exertion of repeatedly turning over an egg timer will cancel out most of your caloric intake, of course.

- The Rice Diet has brought a lot of attention to the importance of this starch in our diet. The Over-Fifty Diet Plan sings the praises of rice, as well. Enjoy a healthy scoop at bedtime, in the form of rice pudding.

- For those of us in our middle years and beyond, oatmeal is especially important. The best sources of oatmeal are oatmeal cookies, oatmeal and raisin cookies (the raisins contain iron, too), oatmeal brownie dessert bars (the chocolate is full of antioxidants and magnesium), and of course, apple crisp (it has oats, and the apples provide vitamins and even more antioxidants).

- Did you know that the right kind of chocolate (the darker, the better) can actually help you lose weight? Dark chocolate contains appetite-suppressant properties that will actually curb your hunger. In fact, you've probably noticed that as you finish off that box of chocolates, you become less and less hungry.

- And finally, remember that trans fats are extremely unhealthy. Don't believe it? Then go to your local bookstore café and read all about them over a slice of New York cheesecake.

Daily Workouts

For years doctors have been recommending a daily exercise program for those of us of the middle-age variety. But I say we're getting plenty of exercise already; we just don't keep track of it.

Here are some exercise programs you're probably already on that you're not even aware of:

The Phone Workout System

- The Macarena moves you do when your cell phone rings and you can't remember which pocket you put it in.
- The double somersault you do when getting out of the shower and slipping on the wet bathroom floor—all in an effort to answer the phone before they hang up.
- The limbo, which you do during church in an effort to crawl under the pew in front of you to hide when your cell phone rings in the middle of the sermon.
- Arm stretches when you're driving and reaching for your ringing cell phone, which is in your purse in the backseat.

The DMV Exercise Program

- Walking from what you discover is the wrong line to what you think to be the right line a minimum of twelve times.
- Knee bends, which you do every time the three-year-old standing in line behind you kicks the back of your leg.
- Walking back to the DMV building after your three-point turn turned into a three-car pileup on your driving test.

The Airline Exercise Program

- Weight-lifting (lifting your barely-under-the-weight-limit luggage into the overhead compartment).
- Sprinting to the farthest possible gate for your connecting flight.
- Leg lifts, as you crawl over the two people in both the aisle and middle seats, while trying to get to your window seat.
- Arm lifts for the security scan (jumping jacks, if you're ticklish).

The above are just three exercise programs that most of us already do. So get out your pedometers and take your pulse. You might be surprised by how much exercise you're already getting throughout your day. And while you're at it, answer that phone!

Pass the Toxins, Please

One of the hottest diets right now is the detox diet. Have you heard about this? I'm not sure how it works, but apparently it involves ridding yourself of all the toxins in your body. Personally, I've always been close with my toxins and don't really know what I would do without them.

Apparently, though, toxins aren't all that good for you. Nice, since supposedly we're getting them in some of the stuff we're eating and breathing every day.

I grew up in Southern California near what was then a major rocket-testing facility. I never thought too much about it, except for the fact that every so often they would run a test that felt a lot like an earthquake. The earth would rumble, and the only way to tell a rocket test from a California earthquake was to look at the light fixtures in the house to see if they were swinging. If they weren't, then it was the rocket-testing site. But if they were swinging enough to keep time to the "Boogie Woogie Bugle Boy," then hit the deck. It could be the big one!

It was a lot of fun growing up in the San Fernando Valley.

Growing up, we never thought much about the smog in Southern California, either. We knew on some days we couldn't see our way to school and our lungs would hurt every time we took a breath, but we just figured everyone else was breathing air that you had to chisel, too.

Now, of course, they tell us that smog isn't a good thing, and they even warn us when the air we're breathing has reached unhealthy levels.

Luckily, I never smoked, but how many people got caught up in that habit before they finally determined that filling your lungs with nicotine probably wasn't a good idea?

So now they're telling us that our bodies have accumulated all of these toxins over the years, and it might be a good idea now to get rid of them.

To do this we're supposed to go on a fast for an allotted number of days. The length of time varies from diet to diet, but they say in order to adequately flush your system, you will need to only drink fluids, or their special concoction, which they'll be more than happy to sell you.

But, come on . . . a liquid diet? Haven't they already punished us enough? Why should we have to give up our food now, too? It doesn't seem fair, does it? They're the ones who didn't warn us about smog, first and secondhand smoke inhalation, nuclear waste, and other things we dealt with as kids. Now they want us to starve?

The ironic thing is, those who have tried the detox diet say that one of the positive byproducts of detoxing your system is an increase in your sense of smell. But what good does it do you to smell a pizza from a hundred yards away if you're on an all-liquid diet?

I'll concede that toxins aren't good for us, and we probably should do something to flush them out of our system. But I'm eating the pizza first.

Eating Our Way to Youth

Speaking of pizza . . .

Many of us would never go to a plastic surgeon by choice. We figure God made us the way we are, so we'll just let nature take its course.

But that was before "anti-wrinkle pizza" hit the market!

That's right—there's a new pizza out now that is being touted as the fountain—or rather, dough machine—of youth. Invented by an Italian nutritionist, this pizza is said to have three times the fiber and more age-defying vegetables and sauce than regular pizza.

What a great idea—*eating our way to a more youthful appearance!* How painless is that? Go ahead and indulge! Eat that double cheese to your heart's content! Order up the pepperoni, the sausage, the mushroom, and yes, the pineapple. Think of it as your edible spa.

But why stop with pizza? Let's make all the foods age-defying. If we could eat our way to a more youthful us, we'd all sign up, right? Toss out those overnight facial creams that send you sliding off your pillow like a seal out of a chute at SeaWorld.

Forget those expensive facial treatments that either burn your face with acid (yeah, that sounds fun) or cut away the excess skin.

Our skin might be falling down on the job, but punishing it by making it endure these procedures is also punishing us. Don't we get that?

But pizza? Who could argue with that? Dual-purposed foods. They've already given us vitamin-fortified snack cakes and cereal. Now, apparently, we can have botox pizza. Okay, maybe it's not Botox, but the result could be the same.

And just think—if food manufacturers put their minds to it, we could also one day have:

Skin-exfoliating cheesecake

Bone-strengthening brownies

Cholesterol-busting snickerdoodles

Blood-pressure-lowering Oreos

Face-lifting fudge

Anti-glaucoma cheese dip

Gout-blocking gooseberry pie

Hair-restoring snow cones

Energy-boosting Bundt cake

Anti-sag chocolate

Think about it—if any of these products were to come on to the market, they would become an overnight success. Store managers wouldn't be able to keep them on their shelves. Shopping cart after shopping cart would be filled to overflowing with these versatile food items. There would be such a run on them, you'd think it was hurricane season all over again.

Obviously, this Italian pizza inventor is on to something. Now my only question is, will he deliver to Tennessee?

One Lump or Two?

I'm not all that happy about the shape I'm in. I didn't used to be in this shape. For most of my life I had more of an hourglass figure . . . with a little less sand where I wanted it and a lot more sand where I didn't want it. But there was still some degree of curvature. I could always count on my waist being located in the general vicinity of where it should be. That was a given. There was enough indentation to refer to it as a waist, and I always knew the approximate area of where to find it.

But that was then, this is now. I no longer have a waist. Or much curvature at all. Today, I am, for lack of a better term, *lumpy*. I'm not talking about big lumps. I'm talking about small lumps. Little lumps of fatty tissue that sort of rise and fall all around the circumference of my body. Some may call this fatty tissue *cellulite* or *fatty deposits*. I call them *flesh waves*. In a swimsuit these waves can make me look like someone outlined my body with a giant pair of pinking shears.

The lumps affect how my clothes hang on me, too. A clingy T-shirt can make me look like I'm carrying two giant strands of ribbon candy on each side under there. Jeans aren't a very flattering fit, either. I have to gather up my lumpiness and push it all upward just to get my jeans to fasten. But there's no place for all that extra skin to go, other than to drop it back down and let it lay there in a mound. I end up looking like an ice-cream cone with a giant scoop of flesh resting on my waistband.

I'm glad looser-fitting styles are in vogue again. Especially loose tops. Do you have any idea how much underarm swag can be tucked into a renaissance-sleeved shirt? Smocks, princess-cut dresses, A-line skirts, and yes, even the muumuu can hide a multitude of buffets.

And flesh waves.

I hated the short-shirt era. It wasn't that long ago when you could hardly find a top that came below your waist. If you raised your arm, everyone could see your belly button—and the accompanying belly. I don't remember asking for that style, do you?

But fashion designers finally got the hint and started lengthening and loosening our fashions. Consider this my thank-you note.

St. John's Dessert Tray

Depressed? In this economy, who isn't? Fortunately there have been studies done on the natural mood-lifting properties in certain foods. Take, for instance, cow's milk. It's been proven that there is a property in cow's milk that helps improve your mood (it's even more potent when it's dripping off an Oreo cookie). Turkey is soothing, too—unless it's served at a Thanksgiving dinner where a family food fight breaks out. In which case, it would depend on how many flying drumstick injuries you end up with.

They say salmon is also a good mood elevator. Not so much for the salmon itself (he's probably pretty ticked off), but to the human eating him. Apparently, there are high levels of vitamin D in salmon, and vitamin D increases the serotonin level in your body. Serotonin makes you feel calmer and happier.

Chocolate also contains serotonin. I figured as much. You don't see too many depressed people with a Hershey's bar hanging out of their mouths. That's because the serotonin lifts your spirits and makes you forget all about your troubles . . . and the calories you're eating.

But what about the rest of the food in our pantries and refrigerators? Maybe there are other foods we should be eating when we're feeling down, food that will lift our moods naturally. And if there are, how do we calculate the dosage we need?

Good question, and one that calls for a chart:

Mood-Lifting Food Chart

Event:	Mood-Altering Food and Dosage:
1. Credit card fee increase	Brownies and a glass of milk per hour until symptoms subside
2. Disagreement with cranky neighbor	One nut roll
3. April fifteenth	A single cherry. (That's all that's left of your hot-fudge sundae after taxes.)
4. Gossiper	One slice of devil's food cake every time you feel your ears burning
5. Baby-sitting eight grandchildren at the same time	One slice of pineapple upside-down cake as soon as you wake up the morning after the sleepover. It will make your house look right-side up again.
6. Fill up at gas station	One 100 Grand candy bar
7. Power outage	One box of Ding Dongs. When the moonlight hits the aluminum foil wrapping just right, it can light up a room and it won't cost you anything.
8. Getting laid off	Two pies, eaten slowly, while looking through Help Wanted ads. (Check with baker to see about mixing pie prescriptions. Some pies don't combine well with other pies, unless washed down with a chocolate shake. There is something in the chocolate shake that seems to neutralize any toxic effects of mixed pie flavors. It's probably the serotonin again.)

9. Unexpected major car repair

One scoop of bread pudding for every $100 between the estimate and the final bill. Add a gallon of ice cream if the mechanic fixed what wasn't wrong with the car and didn't fix what was.

10. Bad haircut

One bag of Tostitos. (For additional mood-lifting benefit, cover head with empty bag.)

Having Your Cake and Eating It, Too

Did you hear a city in New York state recently put a ban on the free donuts that were being given away at their senior center? Talk about living dangerously. Did those city officials or the staff at that senior center realize what kind of jeopardy they were putting themselves in by making such an announcement?

According to reports, the seniors immediately took to the street with picket signs that read "We're old enough to choose!" and "We want our cake and eat it, too!"

For the most part it was a peaceful demonstration. But things could have turned ugly at any moment given the volatility of the situation, and then who's to say the canes and purses wouldn't have started flying?

Frankly, I can't blame those seniors. For years the bakeries were giving them free donuts. They were used to getting free donuts. They wanted their free donuts!

But then, all of a sudden, the donuts were gone. What's up with that?

According to one report, the senior center said they took away the gratis donuts (and pies and breads) in an effort to promote healthier eating habits among its members. But the parents of these seniors are long gone, and many of them don't feel like being parented all over again by either their city government or a senior center board.

If an eighty-year-old man wants a maple bar, that should be his prerogative, shouldn't it? If a ninety-year-old woman wants a custard-filled glazed donut, why's that any of our business? Some of these seniors have spent a lifetime passing on dessert; why should they have to do it in their latter years? This should be the time for them to party hearty, and if that involves a donut in each hand, so be it. If they want a dozen glazed donuts all to themselves, why should anyone else interfere with that ecstasy? There should be a "Don't ask, don't tell. Take your hands off my donut or I'm going to yell!" policy when it comes to seniors and their bakery items.

All you have to do is look at some of the other signs the seniors were sporting in their protest that day to understand their frustration. Signs like "They're carbs, not contraband!" and "Give us our just desserts!" underscore the depth of their dissatisfaction.

I'm not at the age for a senior center yet, but I think if someone had been giving me free bakery goods for years and then suddenly decided to take them all away, I'd have a degree of frustration with that, too. It's not so much the donut part. The free part is what's hard to let go of. That's because as we get older, many of us start calculating these free offers into our budget. Whether it's a freebie that we get on a regular basis, such as the baked goods, or it's trial-size offers of products, two-for-one specials, double grocery store coupons, or all those wonderful senior discounts—they are all considered in our accounting. You can't just take these away without some kind of warning. It's like giving someone a cut in their paycheck. Who would be happy about that?

So give these seniors their donuts back. Let them have their cake and eat it, too. If the city or the senior center is concerned about serving a healthier diet, then fortify the donuts with vitamins. Or use wheat flour. Or serve zucchini or pumpkin muffins instead. Or let them get their vitamins in other foods. But don't just make these fine folks kick their donut habit cold turkey. As a donut connoisseur myself, I can tell you, that's not even human.

Find Strength in Cover Cream

Trendsetting Boomers

Teenagers get a lot of credit (or blame) for being trendsetters. We look at them sporting their funny haircuts and baggy pants and wonder why they can't simply fit in to the "norm." Why do they always have to go against the grain? They do things that we never would have dreamed of doing. (Of course, when we were teenagers, some of us did things our parents never would have dreamed of doing, and our parents did things their parents never would have dreamed of doing. But that's beside the point.)

When it comes to setting trends, though, I am convinced that the world's designers and stylists are overlooking an important group who are breaking new ground in the world of fashion every day. What group is this? The over-fifty crowd, of course.

Think about it—when is the last time you saw a fashion show featuring middle-aged-and-beyond models? You never hear about our "hipness." You don't see us featured on the covers of fashion magazines or modeling on the runways of New York and Paris.

Yet if you sat on a bench at any local mall and watched a few of us parade by, you couldn't help but notice that our age group is a trendsetting force to be reckoned with (our fashion faux pas notwithstanding).

So why are fashion designers all but ignoring us?

I believe it is a case of job security for the twenty-something models, and perhaps even a little jealousy thrown into the mix. If we start getting the attention we deserve and begin calling the shots regarding what's hot and what's not, what will become of the fashionistas of today? They'll lose their power, their influence, and their mega salaries. AARP will start casting *Project Runway*. That's why the youth-driven fashion world likes things just the way they are.

But these designers are missing out on a bonanza of new styles and trends. Those of us over fifty have had a jump on the fashion world for years. And it's not just a replacement hip I'm talking about, either.

No one is paying attention to our styles, though. That is, until some nineteen-year-old dons the exact same outfit, and then all of a sudden it's the newest fad.

Come on, Fifth Avenue, *we had the styles first*! Baggy pants? Grandpas have been wearing those for generations. Multicolored hair? Some senior women have been dying their hair blue for as long as I can remember. Multiple body piercings? We were the first with these, too. What's a new pacemaker and weekly B-12 shots if not body piercings?

It's clear to me that we, the boomer generation, are the ones setting the trends. Yet our styles are being stolen right out from under us, without even a percentage offered!

Now the question is, what are we going to do about it? How can we stop today's fashion industry from undermining our creativity and taking what is rightfully ours?

I say, plenty! We can write letters to these fashion moguls and tell them we're not going to take it anymore! If they don't start giving us our equitable share of the profits, we're going to show up in New York and picket their stores. But all of you men, try not to hike your pants up past your waist when you go. If we're not careful, "High Pants" might be the next hot look for the new season.

We just can't win.

Fashion Faux Pas

Clothing errors continue to be made by the over-fifty crowd in a desperate attempt to look younger. This is not to imply that there is anything wrong with *acting* young at heart. That is perfectly acceptable, and even admirable.

But if we continue to insist on dressing like our teenage grandchildren, it will raise a few eyebrows among our peers (that is, if they haven't had Botox treatments and can therefore still raise their eyebrows).

Because of this unfortunate oversight, and because I want to be as thorough as possible in this area, I am now providing the following:

MIDDLE-AGE FASHION FAUS PAS (Part II)

The following combinations do not go together under any circumstances:

- eyebrow ring and crow's feet
- chest tattoo and a heart monitor

Mohawk   Grandpawk

- ankle bracelet and gout
- bandana and hair plugs
- varicose veins and short shorts
- black toenail polish and hammertoe
- nose ring and nose hairs
- loose-fitting underarm skin and a tight-fitting Def Leppard T-shirt
- metal chains and a muumuu
- low-rise jeans and high-rise granny pants

I'm not saying this is the last word on the subject of appropriate fashion for the middle-aged man or woman. Simply use this as a guideline. It's merely intended to help us all age a little more gracefully.

Once again, so there is no misunderstanding, allow me to restate that I am not talking about the person who *acts* young. Acting young at heart is actually very healthy. It means you're continuing to learn, exercise, change with the times, and participate in creative endeavors. It also means you still know how to have fun with friends and family and enjoy a little more in your day than the evening news and a crossword puzzle.

But dressing too young for your age, especially wearing any of the above fashion combinations, is something you would want to avoid.

If, however, you are already wearing one or more of these combinations, don't be discouraged. Letting go of one's youth is never an easy thing to do. Just ask the man I passed at the mall last week wearing a mohawk toupee. It was downright pitiful.

I've Got the Music in Me

For almost any generation, music is the defining factor. Baby boomers are no exception. Our music spoke of our times, our hopes, our dreams, and of course, that guy or girl we thought we couldn't live without. The passing years, of course, either proved those crushes to be true, or we discovered that we could live without them rather nicely. Whichever way it went, there were songs for both our pain and our ecstasy. There were songs about true love, lost love, broken relationships, lost dogs, desperation, fast cars, and car wrecks in those fast cars. We were singing about surfing, twisting, monster-mashing, and even a dragon named Puff. The music of the boomers covered it all.

Our songs also asked questions like, "Who put the bop in the bop shoo bop shoo bop," and "Who put the ram in the rama lama ding dong?" As far as I know, they're both still a mystery. Most of us are also left wondering what Billy Joe McAllister dropped off the Tallahatchie Bridge.

Just the mere titles of these songs can mentally whisk us away to those good old days. But if we were to sing these songs today, they might have updated titles:

"Waking Up is Hard to Do" (Neil Sedaka)
"Like a Bridge in a Glass of Water" (Simon and Garfunkel)
"Could It Be I'm Falling Again? And Again? And Again?"
    (Spinners)
"Did You Ever Have to Locate Your Mind?" (Lovin' Spoonful)
"Killing Me Softly With His Stairs" (Roberta Flack)
"Deep Heating Number 9" (Coasters)
"50 Ways to Lose Your Buick" (Paul Simon)
"Ain't No Speedbump High Enough to Keep Me From You"
    (Diana Ross)
"Ain't No Grandma Like the One I Got" (Four Tops)
"Goin' to the Rest Home" (Dixie Cups)

Ah . . . let the music play on.

Even with the rewrites, they're still great songs. So load up your iPod (or get your tech-savvy grandkids to do it for you), and start moving to the beat of these classics once again. Move to them during your evening walks, while you're gardening or washing your car, or even while you're walking out to get the mail. It'll do you good, both physically and mentally. And it'll make the neighbors wonder what kind of vitamins you're taking.

The Saggy Sisters Society

No matter how hard we try, we can't fight it. Gravity is here to stay. We have to accept that fact. As we age, parts of us are going to head southward, and there is not a lot we can do about it, outside of surgery.

But even if you manage to take years off your face, you still have to deal with another area of middle-aged drooping. The area I'm referring to is, of course, under the arms.

Frankly, I don't understand the whole underarm sag phenomenon. Why does this happen to us? Did any of us ask for it? Absolutely not!

I can't tell you how many times I've been at the beach and thought a stingray had swam up beside me, only to discover it was just my underarm flesh floating to the surface. This is sad.

Sure, we can try disguising it by pushing the extra flesh up as far as it will go and then secure it with an armband and pass it off as puffy sleeves. But I don't really think it will fool that many people.

We could also try pushing it down to just above our elbows and passing it off as floaties. But that would only work in the pool or at the beach. Most grown women don't wear floaties to the office or formal gatherings.

So if there is no good use for it, why do so many of us have it? Good question.

The first time I noticed my underarm sag was when I was using a hand signal for a left-hand turn and somehow got gravel in the creases of my elbow. *That's odd,* I thought to myself. *How did my elbow reach all the way down to the road?* That's when I had to admit that I had joined my fellow Saggy Sisters and now had my very own Flesh Falls. From that point on, I would need to use extreme caution when wearing tank tops in windstorms.

You know what they say, though . . . good comes out of bad. And from my experience with my own gravity-challenged body, I have decided to form an organization, aptly called The Saggy Sisters Society.

The Saggy Sisters Society is a group of women who have come to terms with their sag. They've got a positive attitude about their sagitude. They know many good women, of varying degrees of sag, have gone before them. People like Eleanor Roosevelt, who said, "The future belongs to those who believe in the beauty of their sag." Or Mae West, who said, "When I'm good I'm very good, but when I sag, I'm better."

I even believe the famous Venus de Milo had this same underarm sag problem. In fact, I'm sure the only reason she's armless is because the sculptor didn't have enough marble for all the extra flesh that she was sporting under there.

So, if the Great Sag has already hit you, don't dismay. You're in good company. A lot of us are dealing with the condition, too. But those of us in the Saggy Sisters Society have gotten to the point where it doesn't really bother us anymore. We're even using it to save money on our air-conditioning bills. (Sit by an open window and the evening breeze will get your underarm flesh moving and circulating the air around, much like a ceiling fan.) But do watch those left-hand turn signals.

No More Ducking

Losing height in our older years usually means weakening bones. That isn't a good thing. But if you could take out the unhealthy part and just leave the shrinkage part, the idea would have some positives—for me, at least. After years of needing to buy Tall Girl clothes, I'd finally be able to shop in the Petite section of department stores. I'd be able to drive a car comfortably without having to stick my head out of the sun roof. And at long last, the top of my head wouldn't be missing from group photos.

I've always been on the tall side. As a baby, I had to hang my feet over the end of my incubator. My legs were so long, they reached the floor when I sat in my high chair. I was one of the tallest girls in high school—even taller than some of the boys. And a few of the teachers.

Being tall comes with its own challenges. Finding jeans and pants that are long enough is never easy. I was wearing Capri-length pants long before they ever became popular. And air travel is no picnic. I usually opt for the aisle seat so I can use the aisle to stretch my legs out, but I get a lot of beverage cart injuries that way.

My mother shrank in her later years. For as long as I could remember, my mom had been a tall woman. But all that changed in her late sixties and early seventies when she began to shrink. By the time she passed away at age seventy-two, she was just a whisper of her former self.

I recall her making comments to me about how much she liked her new petite self. It wasn't a healthy occurrence, of course. She was no doubt losing bone mass. Which was sad, because doctors always told her that she had the bones of a teenager. But she took it in stride. And started shopping for petite sizes.

I think that's what my attitude will be if I ever start shrinking. Don't get me wrong. I'll try to remember to take my calcium and drink plenty of milk to forego any loss of bone mass. But if it happens and one day I notice that I can finally stretch out my legs on an airplane and not kick the elbow of the passenger four rows down, I'll probably be okay with that.

At Long Last Love

I recently heard about a man in Malaysia who had finally found the woman of his dreams. She was 104. He was thirty-three. I believe it was love at first squint.

The groom said he didn't marry his "December bride" for her money, because apparently she doesn't have any. He married her purely for love. And for the way her smile twinkles at him from the nightstand.

It was the groom's first marriage, but the bride's twenty-second! I don't know if her twenty-one previous marriages ended in divorce, or whether she simply outlived them all. At 104, I would imagine she's outlived at least a few of her husbands.

But aren't you curious as to what would make a thirty-three-year-old man marry someone old enough to be his great-great-grandmother? What could two people with that kind of age difference possibly have in common? Do they like the same music? Do they enjoy going to the same places? Who's paying for his vitamins to keep up with her?

I don't know the answer to these questions. All I know is that this couple has to be getting stares when they go for an evening stroll down the street—he on his skateboard, she on her walker.

Don't get me wrong. I'm not saying there's anything wrong with a younger man marrying an older woman. Plenty of men do it, and the practice seems to be gaining in popularity. Older men have been dating younger women for years. Now, it seems, the tables are turning.

One possible reason for this increase in "cougar relationships" is that older women have already made their mistakes in youth and have hopefully learned from them. Older women are usually more mature, too. There's one last benefit, and it could be the very perk this thirty-three-year-old man was looking at with his 104-year-old wife: no mother-in-law.

Beauty Tips on the Cheap

For years, a beauty tip was going around that advocated the use of a popular hemorrhoid cream for under-eye sagging. The drug maker has since issued a warning that their product should be used only for its intended purpose, and is "not for use on the face."

I have to admit, though, I did give this beauty trick a try a few times. I can't really say if it worked or not, but I will tell you that it felt more than a little strange putting hemorrhoid ointment on my face. It was also depressing to realize that I had gotten to a place where the thought of putting hemorrhoid cream on my face even sounded like a good idea. In our search for a new anti-wrinkle cream, have we really stooped this low? No pun intended.

I don't know who first started the rumor that this was an acceptable use of this product. And I'm quite curious as to how they first came up with the idea. Did someone inadvertently get it mixed up with their regular under-eye cream, and then suddenly they noticed they didn't look as tired as they did before?

Whether it works or not, this unconventional use of hemorrhoid ointment is not recommended, and in some cases can be dangerous. That said, it does make you wonder what other ordinary household products might have secondary uses that we're overlooking, doesn't it? Take the following, for example:

Miracle-Gro—What if this could be used as a shampoo, too? Forget hair transplants or expensive hair restoration procedures and medications. Simply go to your local nursery or the garden section of your local big-box discount store and buy yourself some Miracle-Gro. Mix it with your regular shampoo and wait to see what happens. If hair grows, you've saved yourself a fortune. If a crop of corn grows instead, read the disclaimer below.*

Preparation H—Okay, so they've already warned us that it's not for the face. But what if it's safe and would actually work as all-over body cream? Forget those starvation diets, those guilt-inducing, chocolate-bashing, "no deep-fried anything" diets. Instead, slather your plumpish thighs or flaccid belly in a little Preparation H and watch yourself shrink two dress sizes right before your very eyes! Impossible, you say? Perhaps. But what if it's not? What if this unassuming little tube of ointment is the miracle we've all been waiting for? But now, if the cream wears off after so many hours and your size 14 body ends up exploding out of your size 8 dress at a most inopportune time, sending buttons and zipper teeth flying in all directions, please read the disclaimer below.*

Duct tape—It's true that Spanx is the latest rage in slenderizing undergarments. But let's face it, it can be a bit on the pricey side. What if another everyday household product would work just as well? What product? Duct tape, of course. The silver color wouldn't work, but if there were a flesh-colored version, we would all be lining up to shrink-wrap our bodies. And in the case of a serious car wreck or an on-the-job injury, with duct-tape-slenderizing body wrap, we would in essence already have a tourniquet in place. Please read the disclaimer below.*

Wite-Out—We all know that Wite-Out has been worth its weight in gold for years, helping office workers all over the world correct their mistakes. But what if there are other uses for this little jar of paint? What if they were to make this product in a variety of flesh colors that we could match to our own skin tone and use to paint over any blemishes, imperfections, or even varicose veins? Of course, when it dries out and starts chipping away, we could end up looking like we've got some sort of strange fungus. But it might be worth it. See disclaimer below.*

Brillo pads—Why buy a loofah sponge when you've got a Brillo pad just sitting there under your sink, not doing anything between meals? These pads even come with their own soap! See disclaimer below.*

Lava soap—Most of us middle-agers can remember the thrill of washing our hands with Lava. Nothing could get off dirt, grime, and the first layer of skin like this little wonder bar. But what if Lava is good for other things? Like stripping the varnish off old furniture, or priming that classic '62 Impala for a new paint job. Forget Derma Peels. Just use Lava. Please read disclaimer below.*

Look around your house. You'll probably come up with plenty of other ideas on your own. There must be hundreds of other household products just waiting to be used to their full potential. So be creative. Enjoy. But read the disclaimer below first.

*The use of any of the above-mentioned products for any purpose other than its intended use is neither recommended nor endorsed. The above suggestions are for entertainment purposes only. Then again, if any of them work . . .

Live to Annoy

Red Tape

Every once in a while you'll read about the Social Security Department or some insurance company rejecting a person's benefits due to an error in their paper work that inadvertently lists the person as dead, when they're not. Apparently, this is not that simple of a matter to clear up.

If it ever happens to me, I know I'd have a difficult time proving my existence. First, to be declared alive, you need to have a pulse. Since not everyone can find my pulse, this could go against me.

Another way to prove you're alive is to be breathing. I can't always prove this, either. Sometimes when I doze off during the evening news, I don't appear to be breathing. Until someone changes the channel.

You see the dilemma? It's not that easy to prove one's existence. You could find yourself drowning in a sea of red tape, working your way up the chain of command, while supervisor after supervisor refuses to admit your existence.

I heard about a man who was actually elected to a political office after he had died. Now, some elected officials have acted lifeless after they've gotten into office, but electing a deceased person into office on purpose is probably rare. It also doesn't speak very highly of the guy who lost the election to a dead guy.

Some celebrities have had premature reports of their death. It happened to Bob Hope twice. One of the reports was picked up off an Associated Press Web site and announced on the floor of the House of Representatives by Arizona Republican Congressman Bob Stump.

"It is with great sadness," he said, "I announce that Bob Hope has died."

Meanwhile, Bob was sitting happily at home having breakfast. This was five years before his actual death.

It happened to Mark Twain, too. His reply was, "Reports of my death have been greatly exaggerated."

Alfred Nobel, benefactor of the Nobel Prize, is said to have created the prizes after reading his premature obituary. The fact that he had been called a "merchant of death" for inventing dynamite bothered him. So he spent the rest of his life making sure there would be more positive things to say about him after his death.

So if you're ever faced with similar circumstances, if you ever have to prove your existence when insurance companies, news reports, or government agencies are saying otherwise, you'll need to know how to prove you're alive.

After much thought, I've come up with a few ideas that might help:

Ten Ways to Prove That You're Alive

1. Since many of us look dead in our driver's license photos, these might not be the best government identification to provide. Instead, show your health club photo ID card. The shock of the price of a three-year membership will usually give your photo that wide-eyed look. If the agency still doesn't believe you, try #2.

2. Breathe on a mirror. Most government bureaucracies are familiar with hot air and will accept this as proof of your existence. If they don't, move on to #3.

3. Let someone from the agency take your pulse, but not a blood sample. If they are a legitimate government agency, they'll only require your blood every April 15. If your pulse is too faint, or they simply don't believe you have one, then move on to #4.

4. Have your book club give you a reference. No book club has ever mistakenly listed someone as dead. In fact, some will continue to send monthly book offers for up to fourteen years after someone's demise. And even then, the death has to be certified, with no less than four respected medical opinions. If this doesn't work, continue to #5.

5. Have your wife vouch for you. She may have already had years of experience convincing her mother that you're not a dead weight. But if the agency still won't take her word for it, move on to #6.

6. Miss a car payment. The calls and letters from your loan company should give you more than enough proof that you're alive.

7. Have your doctor give you a letter. If you still owe her money for your last office or hospital visit, she'll definitely vouch for your pulse.

8. Forget to pay a traffic ticket, then ignore the reminders. You'll soon get a letter from a judge that will more than prove your existence.

9. Have your pastor send a letter. Despite the comatose appearance you may have had during a few recent services, he would probably be more than happy to help you prove your existence.

10. Show them the receipt for this book. Most people don't read that much after death.

Smart Chips . . . and Dip

The idea of implanting identification chips into human beings is no longer a plot of science fiction movies. The technology is already here.

These ID chips could feasibly contain all your pertinent information, including but not limited to name, address, phone number, medical history, credit report, names and ages of children, address and phone number of a relative not living with you, your high school GPA, your SAT score, your batting average on your Little League team, two-for-one dining coupons, an index of all your PINs and passwords, your great-grandmother's maiden name, and the date of your last oil change.

Now, as convenient as it might be to have such information virtually at your fingertips, or wherever else they insert it, the whole idea is a little disconcerting, isn't it? We think the airport security is tough to get through now. Just wait until people are trying to get through with these chips surgically implanted in them.

"Excuse me, sir, would you mind stepping over here while I wand your ID chip? We believe we're picking up an overdue library book from the '80s."

Maybe it's just me, but the whole ID chip concept sounds a little too Big Brother-ish. Or end-of-the-world-ish. The only chips I want in my body are the ones from Frito-Lay.

Do we really want the following scenes taking place:

"It says here that you had spinal meningitis back in 1953. We don't think it's a good idea for you to fly on this airplane. Luckily, we haven't reached our cruising altitude yet; we're only ten thousand feet in the air. Good-bye."

Or, *"Excuse me, but it says here that you were involved in a political demonstration in 1972. We don't think we want you working for our company. We here at Fat Willie's burgers pride ourselves in not supporting any viewpoint. Here's your pink slip and your severance soda."*

To be fair, though, there are other uses for this kind of technology that wouldn't intrude on our personal privacy but would, instead, serve the public. Take, for instance, the important-dates chip. This warning chip would be implanted into a man's wrist to sound an alarm on the morning of his anniversary, Valentine's Day, or his wife's birthday. It would continue sounding the alarm every hour throughout the day until he successfully wands the barcode of a suitable gift over the chip. Think of the marriages it could save!

For those of us on diets, a dessert chip would be good. It could be implanted in our chin (any one of them) and would warn us whenever a dessert is getting dangerously close. With the dessert-chip implant, a waiter wouldn't be able to get that dessert tray within viewing distance without the alarm going off.

Some football fans might not mind having an information chip inserted in their body to hold their team stats. It would keep them up-to-date on the wins, losses, draft picks, and latest scandals.

Like I said, though, I still feel a little uneasy about it all. Having a chip under my skin that knows more about me than I do is just too weird. Besides, the way my skin's going, it could start out on my neck and end up down by my ankles in no time.

The Baby Boomer's "How Long Will You Live?" Test

There is a wide assortment of tests available now that can provide you with a way to calculate (approximately, of course) how long you will live. These tests factor in your various lifestyle choices and habits in an effort to determine whether these are adding or subtracting years from your life.

These tests are fun, but many of them are hard to follow or are too vague in their questions.

The following test is neither. It is simplistic and a much more fun way to find out how your lifestyle is affecting your chance of living a long life.

Get out your pencils, please. . . .

You will begin with today's average age span of approximately seventy-seven years, and then deduct or add to that age according to your answers to the following:

1. Do you typically turn the wrong way down a one-way street because you believe in "going against the flow"? If the answer is yes, take away four years.

2. Do you consider the speed limit merely a "starting point"? If your answer is yes, take away three years.

3. Do you wait until you can see the headlights of the eighteen-wheeler coming toward you before you decide to pass that Geo Metro that's going at a snail's pace in front of you? If the answer is yes, take away five years.

4. Do you keep a toaster by your bathtub just in case you want a snack? If your answer is yes, take away 3.2 years.

5. When crossing a busy intersection, do you have the attitude that the cars will stop when they see you? (You're wearing your lucky black shirt, and that should cancel out any danger, right?) If the answer is yes, take away 2.7 years.

6. Do you consider Crisco a food group? If your answer is yes, take away 1.8 years.

7. Have you ever dropped a frozen turkey into a deep fryer just to see how high the flames would go? If your answer is yes, take away two years.

8. Have you ever said to yourself, "That looks like a thundercloud. I think I'll go golfing"? If the answer is yes, take away 2.3 years.

9. Is your favorite snack buttered pork rinds? If your answer is yes, take away 3.1 years.

10. Have you ever fallen asleep while laying out in the summer sun, and didn't wake up until you could smell your flesh sizzling? If your answer is yes, take away 4.2 years.

As you can see, unwise choices will have a detrimental effect on your life expectancy. So if this test has revealed that you'll end up living fewer years than you would like, do something to change your habits today.

Or if you feel fine about your choices, then just grab some buttered pork rinds and move on to the next chapter. . . .

Son, Can I Borrow the Car?

*"I was always taught to respect my elders,
and I've now reached the age when I don't have
anybody to respect."*

George Burns

Sometimes you might find yourself needing to borrow your son's or daughter's car. This happens to all of us. But you should know that before they hand over the keys, they will put you through nothing short of the Spanish Inquisition. After requiring their folks, the two people who birthed them—the ones who fed, burped, and changed their diapers—to fill out an Offspring Vehicle Request Form, as well as all pertinent proof of insurance forms AND providing a minimum of three references, some of these adult children of baby boomers will hold their car keys in the air (like you would do to a cocker spaniel) and make their parents beg to borrow their car. Never mind that these parents probably used the same tactic on them when they were teenagers; it's the principle of the thing.

Besides, just look at all the classic cars that are still around today. That's proof positive that we know how to drive and take care of a car. Forget those street-dragging scenes you might have seen on films like *American Graffiti* or in old Steve McQueen films. We've made it this far, so we must be doing something right behind the wheel. In fact, most of us taught our offspring how to drive. We may have even bought them their first car or paid for their insurance. So where is all of this automotive hostility coming from?

Power. That is what has to be driving it. Our grown kids finally have us where they want us. They've been waiting for years to get even for what they've perceived as unfair curfews, forced homework, and after-hours phone calls abruptly unplugged.

Granted, it could also be that some of us have abused our rights to borrow the cars of our sons or daughters (one accidental plunge into a lake and they never forget it).

Whatever the reason, this is an area of parent-offspring interaction that is primed for hurt feelings and misunderstandings.

So if your son or daughter isn't letting you borrow their car due to trust issues, then I am providing the following list of do's and don'ts in an effort to help repair the broken trust.

When borrowing your grown son's or daughter's car, it is important to:

1. Never misplace or lose the key. (If you do, at least try to recall what county you were in when you lost it. Saying "Somewhere in Georgia" is not sufficient. It will do little to convince your offspring to ever let you borrow the car again.)

2. Ponds are for ducks. And paddle boats. Don't forget that. It does not matter that your navigational program says to continue driving straight. If you are looking at a pond in front of you, chances are it is probably there. It is not a road. Roads typically do not go through ponds. Ignore your navigational system. Pond water has a distinctive odor that is very difficult to get out of upholstery, which is another reason not to continue driving straight into the pond. Because of this foul odor, you will not be able to convince your children that the wet seats are due to a detailed car wash.

3. Always look behind you before backing up. This will reduce your risk of running into abandoned shopping carts. Or a giant billboard.

4. Do not drive the wrong way down a one-way street, even if it is a shortcut to the YMCA. Your offspring will not want to hear about the benefits of your exercise program while at the same time hearing that their car has been totaled in a head-on collision with a mail truck. The latter will always take precedence.

5. No matter how many crumpled Stop signs you have seen, their primary purpose is not to *physically* stop your car. You are supposed to stop *before* the limit line, not after you've crashed into the sign. If you do run into a Stop sign, however, do not forget to remove the remnants of the sign from the roof of your car before returning the vehicle to your offspring. This is the polite and responsible thing to do.

6. Do not get the car stuck in mud. If you do, you might want to leave out the part about going off-roading with the Red Hat Ladies.

7. Do fill up the car with gas before returning it to your offspring. It may involve taking a second loan out on your home (if you can get one these days), but it's still the right thing to do.

8. When raising the driver's seat so that you can see over the steering wheel, remember to lower it again so that your six-three son doesn't inadvertently install a new sun roof with his head the next time he climbs into his car.

9. If you drove down any back roads in their car, it's polite to wash the insect residue and bird droppings off of the windshield before returning the car. This would also include any deer you happened to hit. Again, it's the polite thing to do.

10. If you are going to switch the radio dial to a classical music station and then turn up the dial full blast so you can hear

it, be sure NOT to readjust the volume before returning the car. I repeat, DO NOT readjust the volume before returning the car. This is considered fair payback for all those garage band practices that you had to put up with during your child's teen years.

Bickering Could Be Hazardous to Your Health

According to a report in the *Journal of Gerontology* (November 2005 issue), bickering couples tend to heal more slowly.

That actually makes sense when you think about it. If you've been arguing with your wife, and she just so happens to be changing the dressing on your foot wound, chances are pretty good that your wound is going to heal more slowly . . . especially if she's applying hot sauce to it instead of Bactine!

So, yes, it's probably true that having a healthy, happy relationship with your spouse can cause your own body to function better. In fact, the following chart, computed from interviews with hundreds—okay, several—of my married friends, is provided to help you see exactly how this concept works:

Bickering incident	Result	Delay in Healing
Fight over who's hogging the blanket	Whiplash from blanket being suddenly yanked away from you in the middle of the night	Extra two weeks to heal
Disagreement over the thermostat setting	Carpal tunnel syndrome from repetitive motion of lowering the thermostat immediately after husband raises it	Extra month to heal
Bickering over unhealthy diet	Lump on head after spouse bonks you on your noggin for not having a V-8	Extra four days to heal
Arguing over the finances	Smoke inhalation from dynamiting credit cards	Extra two weeks, including one week in oxygen tent
Visit from in-laws	Carpel tunnel syndrome from hours of plugging ears to keep from hearing how much better their daughter or son could have done	Could be an extra three weeks, depending on length of visit
Whose turn it is to do the dishes	Lower back injury from repeated ducking to keep dinnerware from scoring a direct hit	Extra two months of physical therapy
Forgotten anniversary	Sciatic nerve damage from sleeping on sofa	Injury could last one year until your next anniversary, at which time you will have the chance to redeem yourself and improve your chances of a full recovery

Backseat driving	Severe pain in the neck	Pain will last until you arrive at your destination, with recurring pain each time trip is recalled
Getting lost, but not stopping to ask for directions	Severe vertigo from going around in circles	Extra two-week recovery period for vertigo to subside and GPS to be installed
Dirty socks left on the floor	Broken ankle, if sock had been lying there for more than eight days and stiffened to the texture of petrified wood, causing you to trip on it, executing a perfect double somersault over the coffee table	An extra six weeks, with leg elevated on petrified sock

So, yes, as you can see, bickering couples do heal more slowly. If you've got a wound that just won't heal, maybe it's time to look at how well you and your spouse are getting along. Or take a taste of the Bactine. If it tastes like something you should be putting on a taco, you might want to start changing the dressing yourself.

Calling All Grouches

Recently there has been a lot of talk about becoming friends with your "inner child." That can be a good thing. But what about your "inner grouch"? Is anyone paying him or her any attention? And what about that constant battle that goes on between your inner child and your inner grouch? Some days it's relentless, "Grow up!" "Don't grow up!" "Grow up!" "Don't grow up!" No wonder those of us over fifty have to buy so much antacid.

Your inner child may want to plant a garden while your inner grouch wants to hurl clumps of dirt at the neighborhood kids who walk across your lawn. Your inner child may want to toss a football around, but your inner grouch wants to throw a football at the television screen during the evening news.

It's a constant emotional tug-of-war.

October 15 has officially been named National Grouch Day. I don't know who decided that particular day would be the perfect day to recognize grouches, but it must have been someone who ran into a grouch on October 15 and decided that we might as well honor these grumpy gooses if we're going to have to deal with them. After all, there have to be some positive aspects to grouchy people.

I believe I've found a few. . . .

If a grouchy waiter can upset you so much that you get up and leave before your meal arrives, think of all the calories he's saving you. Not to mention the tip.

If you run into a grumpy Santa Claus who doesn't promise your grandkids a single thing, think of all the money he'll be saving you this Christmas.

If that international travel agent you're dealing with is a grouch, you might just decide to stay home and tour the local sites for a change. At the price of airline tickets today, that's a real gift.

If that clerk at the mall is nasty, you might get so irritated that you put back all the stuff you couldn't really afford to buy anyway.

If that car dealer is rude and inconsiderate, you might change your mind about buying a new car and stay with your faithful, paid-off old beater for a little while longer.

If that door-to-door salesman who just interrupted your dinner has a bit of an attitude, then you won't have any feelings of guilt when you tell him "No, thank you" and shut the door.

If that hospital nurse is a little put out every time you ring for her, it's going to drive you to get well more quickly so you can get back to your own home.

If another driver honks her car horn and yells at you for going too slowly, it'll make you slow down even more in front of her. That could be a good thing. There are very few fatal car crashes at five miles per hour.

If a grouchy Realtor acts like you're bothering him or her every time you call with a question, think how much money you'll save by selling the house yourself.

See, there are lots of benefits to having grouches in your life. But don't be a grouch yourself. Why? Grouches don't have a lot of friends; snarling increases wrinkles; and in this day of economic uncertainty, it's best to keep our two cents for ourselves.

So be on guard. Your inner grouch can creep up on you when you least expect it, especially the older you get. For now, let your inner child—the part of you that loves to have fun—come out to play as often as possible.

While visiting a convalescent home some years ago, I met one particular patient in the hallway who, to this day, still stands out in my mind. She had the sweetest smile I had ever seen. She was wheelchair-bound, as were many of the other patients. But you wouldn't know she had any limitations at all by looking at her face. She didn't have any visitors that day, also like so many of the other patients. But you wouldn't know it by the twinkle in her eye. She smiled at everyone who walked by her in the hallway, and she would try to engage them in conversation. She clearly wasn't allowing her circumstances to hold her back. She saw everyone who walked through those doors as a potential friend. Or someone she could trip, and then giggle and pretend she didn't do it. She had a sweet, mischievous air about her. I found myself looking forward to seeing her every time I visited there.

We have a choice when it comes to how joyful we're going to be in this life. We may not have a choice when it comes to the problems that cross our path, but we do have a choice in our attitude about them. This woman looked to be in her eighties, and I'm sure in that amount of time she experienced plenty of disappointments. She may have outlived a husband. Maybe she even outlived a son or daughter. Only she and God know all the chapters in her life story. But one thing was evident: She was bound and determined to have a happy ending.

They're Baaaaaack!

The reasons they do it are varied. Maybe they just graduated from college and are waiting to land that dream job. Maybe they've just gone through a painful divorce and need their family's emotional and spiritual support at this transitional time in their life. Maybe they do it so they can save up money for a home purchase. Or maybe they do it for a hundred other reasons.

What is it they're doing?

Moving back home.

Also called *boomeranging*, it's when adult children move back home. But with a little adjustment, consideration, and mutual respect, boomerang situations can be a positive experience. They can also provide you with plenty of good memories, heart-to-heart talks, and that good feeling, knowing you're giving your son or daughter an often much-needed second chance at life. Before you know it, they'll be back on their feet and thriving.

But you as the parents will need to remember that it is another adult living with you now, not your fifteen-year-old. That is not an easy change to make in your state of mind. For one thing, the usual mom-isms or dad-isms either don't work, or they desperately need a rewrite once your offspring has passed the twenty-one, thirty-one, or in some cases, the forty-one-year-old mark. With older adult children, your interaction sounds a little more like this:

"Don't make me make you pull this car over!"
"It's no use crying over spilled Starbucks."
"Turn down that business channel! I can't even hear myself think!"
"If all your friends got Botox, would you do it, too?"

See, it's not the same, is it?

Another factor facing the boomerang household is space. When grown children move back home, they tend to show up with a lot more stuff than they originally left with. In fact, you can usually tell a boomerang home simply by looking at the furnishings. What other household has two complete sofa sets in the living room, twin toasters in the kitchen, and an extra six dining room chairs spread strategically throughout the house? The upside to this, of course, is you have plenty of seating for your Small Group meeting.

What you lose in space, though, you gain in laundry. But don't worry. You might not have to be the one doing it. That's because during their time on their own they have developed their own style of folding (it's no longer the ball they preferred in high school). In fact, they might not even want you touching their clothes. There's too big of a risk for your clothes to get mixed up with theirs. (It's the multi-generational baggy-pants dilemma again. They don't want Grandpa's baggy pants getting mixed up with their baggy pants. Either that or they don't like how the odor of their Brut mixes with the scent of the deep-heating rub residue on your clothes.)

Curfew is a problem that might need to be addressed. It's hard to tell a thirty-year-old man or woman that they need to turn off the television so you can go to sleep. But eight o'clock is eight o'clock!

Choice of television shows can be another source of disagreement with a boomerang son or daughter. For some reason The Weather Channel doesn't rank as high on their entertainment list as it does on ours.

But if you happen to find yourself in the path of a tornado or hurricane, I'm sure they'll let you turn to The Weather Channel. At least until the TV set gets blown out the window.

STEP SEVEN:

Choose to Keep Going

Ten Money-Saving Tips for Today's Economy

By this age, most of us are on a fixed budget. We're either living on our retirement checks or we're saving aggressively for our retirement. Because of this, we're always looking for additional ways to save. This is especially true when the economy is down. Anything we can do to shave a little off our expenses, we're more than willing to try.

Here are a few money-saving tips I can suggest:

1. Vacation at home this summer. Not just in your hometown. I mean, *at home*. If you calculate how much money you're losing in this housing crisis, your home may be costing you more per day than some four-star hotels. So spend as much time in your house as you can. Take some of the sting out of that adjustable mortgage by creating new memories within those walls. If you can talk your family into providing room service, all the better. And if you've always wanted to go on an Alaskan Cruise for personal enlightenment, try the frozen-food aisle in the grocery store.

2. Grow your own garden. Gardening is a relaxing hobby. It'll also help with your grocery budget. And just think, by growing your own vegetables, you won't have to worry about what

will be on the next salmonella recall list. You might want to buy a cow, too, as long as your homeowners' association doesn't mind. And your condo patio is big enough.

3. Call your credit card companies and ask them to lower your interest rate. If they will, you'll save yourself a lot of money. If they won't, write the Federal Reserve, who is looking in to these ridiculously high interest rates that credit card companies are charging, and add your complaint to the growing list. That'll save you a lot of money in therapy.

4. Skip bottled water and sodas. Go back to drinking regular tap water. This goes for when you're eating out, too. Not eating out is the best money saver, but if you must do it, then at least pass on ordering a two-dollar beverage. Over the course of a year, you'll save a small fortune.

5. Again, if you're going to eat out, then by all means, choose buffets. If there are no policies against this, time your arrival so that you're there at the feeding troughs between meals. That way you can eat breakfast *and* lunch or lunch *and* dinner.

6. Skip the beach this summer. Simply apply a good tanning lotion, and then sit in your convertible in your driveway. It'll give you that beach look, without the expense of a road trip to get there. (Be careful to avoid steering-wheel tan lines.)

7. Never idle your car's engine. This wastes precious gas. Instead, turn off the engine while waiting in all drive-through lanes and at red lights. Who cares if the person behind you has to wait an additional millisecond for you to start your engine? You'll be helping them to slow down in life and saving your own gas in the process. It's a win-win for both of you. Of course, if they get out of the car and punch you out, your medical expenses could override your fuel savings. But with the price of gas these days, it still might be worth the risk.

8. Cut your own hair. So what if your hand slips and you shave off one side? You can always join a rock band and pretend you meant to cut it that way.

9. Hold a garage sale and turn all those unwanted items into cold, hard cash. In this economic downturn, it might be time to let go of that armadillo lamp.

10. Cut out coupons and, more important, remember to use them. If the person in line behind you has to watch his milk expire while each one of your 137 coupons are entered into the register, then so be it. Again, you're helping him slow down in life (refer to tip #7), and you're saving big bucks on your grocery bill in the process.

These are only ten ways to help your money stretch in today's economy. Feel free to add a few of your own. In the long run, your wallet will thank you for it. And as for that armadillo lamp, now that I think about it, I do have an empty end table that could use a new accent piece. How much are you asking?

This story originally appeared on New Christian Voices, *www.newchristianvoices.com/column/marthas-laugh-lines-10-money-saving-tips-todays-economy*, July 22, 2008.

How High Will It Go?

I remember the day when five dollars used to buy a full tank of gas. Now if you pump five bucks on pump 3, it's just enough to get you over to pump 6 for more!

Some people believe this problem of soaring gasoline prices could be eased if only the CEOs of the petroleum companies would take a cut in their annual salaries. But I don't know. It may not be that easy to get by on only $102 million a year!

There is an e-mail currently circulating the Internet that is supposed to help us feel better about paying these escalating fuel prices. The e-mail compares the price of gas to the price of other things, such as Wite-Out at $25.42 a gallon, Pepto Bismol at $123.20 a gallon, and printer's ink at $5,200 a gallon. (I can understand why they're bringing up the price of Pepto Bismol, because with the fluctuating price of gasoline, we're all drinking so much of it!)

But it works the other way, too. The same five dollars that we could one day be paying for a gallon of gasoline could also buy:

2,500 gallons of tap water (and that's not even counting the value of all the lead particles in it)

4,500 meters of thread
8,000 toothpicks
25,000 staples
4 pounds of popcorn kernels
4 pounds of corn meal
500 sheets of paper
1,200 paper clips

So what's the point? Five bucks for a gallon of gasoline is still five bucks, no matter what you compare it to.

All this makes the days of the cowboys look pretty good, doesn't it? Cowboys could travel for weeks going from watering hole to watering hole, and it didn't cost them a cent.

Or we could even compare it to the Bible days. Jesus and his disciples walked almost everywhere they went. Check out your Bible maps and I guarantee you won't find a single SUV dealership listed on any of them. Their mode of transportation was primarily their own feet, but according to their travel log, as recorded in the Bible, it certainly didn't slow them down any.

So maybe we should take a cue from all of them and get out of our cars and walk a little more. It's healthy for us, and it might go a long way toward getting these gas prices to start coming down. But I'd recommend buying a good pair of sandals first. And you might want to leave a couple days early for work.

This story originally appeared on New Christian Voices, *www. newchristianvoices.com/column/how-high-will-it-go*, May 5, 2008.

A Matter of Will

It's interesting, isn't it, how creative, vindictive, generous, petty, controlling, enabling, negligent, thorough, and empowering some people can get in the writing of their wills. For some people, it's like they're wanting to get in the last word, even if they do it from the great beyond. For others, it's a matter of making sure they're still in control, even after death. And then there are those who simply want their wishes carried out for the noblest and most loving reasons.

Let's look at "control" and "getting in the last word" first. You may have heard about the late Leona Helmsley who left her dog some $12 million. Trouble—that's the dog's name—is a very well-to-do Maltese now, thanks to the provision Leona made for him in her will. Trouble will continue to live his life in the style to which he was accustomed, under the supervision of Leona's brother, Alvin. Leona also left two of her grandchildren five million dollars each (with the stipulation that they visit the grave of their father at least once a year). The other two grandchildren got, let me see . . . oh yeah, zip.

I don't know why Leona decided to leave these two grandchildren out of her will. According to the wording in the document, they already should know why. Whether they actually do or not apparently wasn't her concern.

Grandparents' Day must have been loads of fun at the Helmsley's, huh?

But before we judge Leona too harshly, let's be quick to realize that she isn't the only one who's ever done this sort of thing. The news and history books are full of these kinds of last-will-and-testament stories.

One billionaire, Ruth Lilly, of the Eli Lilly pharmaceutical fortune, is bequeathing some one hundred million dollars to a struggling poetry magazine that had—get this—*rejected her multiple times*! One hundred million dollars in exchange for *rejection letters*! Talk about getting in the last word!

The story is that the magazine, *Poetry*, consistently returned the eighty-seven-year-old's poems, which she had continually submitted over the years, telling her the works were "not suitable for publication." I'm pretty sure her check will not be returned in like manner.

Ed Headrick, the man known for perfecting and patenting the Frisbee and who once remarked, "When we die, we don't go to purgatory. We just land up on the roof and lay there," had a special last request, too. Ed loved his product so much that he wanted his ashes to be molded into Frisbees. This sort of brings new meaning to singing "I'll Fly Away" at a funeral, doesn't it? I understand that you can now buy Ed Headrick memorial Frisbees for several hundred dollars—and yes, some of Ed is in each one.

I wonder if the inventor of the Hula-Hoop requested his ashes be put in his product, too; you know, so he could go around a few more times.

I recently read about a man in Portugal who flipped through his city's phone book to find seventy complete strangers among whom to divide his sizeable estate. (Sort makes you reconsider the benefits of an unlisted number, doesn't it?)

Last wishes, wills, final requests—we don't like to talk about them, but they're an important part of life. Especially if you want your final wishes carried out.

Have you given much thought to what you would write in your will? Now, have you given much thought to what you would write in your will *if you knew you could get away with it*? Here are a few things I think would be fun to include in mine:

- To the friend who talked me into sky diving at that discount sky diving company (should that be the way I go), I leave my booklet of discount coupons for return visits.

- To the relative who, when I was in the hospital unable to move or talk and could only listen, left all the musical Get Well cards open and going off simultaneously, I bequeath diddley squat.

- To whoever hires the mariachi band to perform the hat dance at my funeral receives an automatic 20 percent cut in their inheritance.

- To whichever relative suggests passing on the normal casket for the box that the Foosball table came in last Christmas, I leave zilch.

- To anyone who (should I succumb to some fatal disease) did not believe I was truly sick and made the comment, "Snap out of it, whiner," receives one dollar and a copy of all of my health records.

- To anyone who insists that I would want to be buried in any bridesmaid dress I have ever worn, I leave nothing.

- To the jokester who thought it would be funny to tuck a cell phone under my funeral pillow and then call it during the funeral services, I leave a hundred bucks (you've got to reward creativity like that).

- To the person who (should this be my demise) said, "It's just a spider bite," I leave nothing, save my copy of *Arachnophobia*.

- To the individual who (should this be my end) said, "It's just a Stephen King film. What's it going to do? Scare you to death?" I leave zip.

- And finally, to the one who didn't spell-check my tombstone and let it be engraved with the words, "May She Rest in Peas," I leave nada . . . well, except for a dictionary.

Survivors

Any of you who are over the age of fifty can put this book down right now and give yourself a pat on the back. With both hands. Why? Because you've survived!

Surviving into your fifties, sixties, and beyond isn't for the weak of mind. It takes a certain amount of grit, determination, and an ability to adapt to your ever-changing circumstances.

Generations past may have had their Great Depression, World Wars I and II, and the Civil War. But our generation has had its own share of wars and disasters to deal with. If you're a baby boomer you've survived a lot. You've seen the assassination of a president, the attempted assassination of two others, real estate and stock market booms and busts, and decades full of other traumatic and amazing things.

You've witnessed/survived/enjoyed the following:

Disco
The Macarena
The Beatles
The Bay of Pigs
The Edsel

The John Kennedy assassination
The Bobby Kennedy assassination
The rise and fall of the Berlin Wall
The end of the Cold War
Hurricane Katrina
The first man on the moon
The Vietnam War
Cassius Clay/Muhammad Ali
Patti Hearst
Star Trek
The Martin Luther King Jr. assassination
The Nixon resignation
The Clinton impeachment attempt
Perry Mason
My Mother, The Car
Star Wars
The word *groovy*
Tiny Tim
Elvis's death and reported later "sightings"
Undergarment burnings
Go-go boots
Twiggy
Dr. Ben Casey
The Munsters
Pet rocks

The list can go on and on. The point is, we've lived. And we've survived. We've participated in life and rose to the occasion whenever we needed to. That's a life well lived. We can look back on it and be thankful for the lessons we've learned, the laughs we've shared, and the good friends and memories we've made through it all.

Letters to Old Friends

Lately I've been receiving letters from the families of old friends asking me to write a memory for their birthday or anniversary. I love doing this sort of thing. It's fun to sit down and reminisce about the good times of life, isn't it? The belly laughs you've shared, the ups, the downs, the tears, the births, the "raising a teenager" years, the weddings, the vacations, the funerals, the joys, the pains, the memories—in other words, the journey.

Old friends will always bring a smile to your face and a warm feeling to your heart. My husband and I spend a lot of time thinking about our old friends—friends who have stood the test of time, who have been all-weather friends, not just good-weather friends. So I've written them a letter. . . .

> *To you, old friend:*
>
> *It's been a long time since we first said "Hello." Had I known then what I know now—what a faithful, fun friend you would turn out to be—I probably would have made greater note of it in my journal. (Had I kept a journal back then.)*
>
> *I may not tell you often enough, or maybe I've never told you at all, but my life is easier because you're in it. You've been*

my encourager, my cheerleader, someone to laugh with and cry with; you've been a rock. Whenever I've doubted myself, you've made me doubt those doubts by reminding me of my worth.

I've whined to you and may have even monopolized the conversation when you had your own pain. I'm sorry for that.

Thank you for the advice you've given to me, both when I've asked for it and when I haven't. You've been a wise counselor, and you've never charged me a dime.

It doesn't matter whether we first met in junior high or high school, whether it was at work, church, a service organization, or wherever it was that our paths first crossed; as far as I'm concerned, it was a day orchestrated by God himself. He knew that I would need a friend like you in my life. And he saw to it that it happened.

I hope I've been that kind of friend to you.

Life's hard; friends soften the blows.

Miles may separate us, or you may live close enough that I could walk to your house for a cup of tea. It doesn't matter. Our friendship has stood the test of time. Just like I always knew it would.

Thanks for being a part of my life and making it richer.

A grateful old friend.

Those Three Little Words

"Life's greatest happiness is to be convinced
we are loved."
Victor Hugo

Most of us love hearing those three little words, "I love you." They can make our day, can't they? We all want to be loved.

There are three other words that we hear a lot, too, and that's "How are you?"

Sometimes those three words are spoken sincerely. Sometimes they're not. Sometimes the person saying them doesn't even wait for a response. They just walk on, or they'll dive into a recounting of all their own problems, without even acknowledging that you might have any.

Like "I love you," the words "How are you?" are better when they're heartfelt. "How are you?" is a question, not a statement. If someone is going to take the time to ask the question, they need to wait for the answer.

Perhaps the reason they don't wait is because the answer is often not genuine, either. People answer with "Fine" when their life is in shambles. They'll say they're "Great" when their daughter just dropped out of school or their son has run away from home. Again. They'll say "Couldn't be better" when they're flat broke and they could, in fact, be a whole lot better.

I'm not talking about having a positive attitude in the face of difficult circumstances. That's a good thing. Like these positive responses:

"How are you?"
"Above ground."
—Old Southern saying

"How are you?"
"Better than I deserve."
—Dave Ramsey, radio financial talk-show host

"How are you?"
"All in all, I'd rather be in Philadelphia."
—President Ronald Reagan, on his way into surgery following an assassination attempt

I once read someone answer the question "How are you?" with this:

"Vertical and ventilating."

Those are wonderfully upbeat responses to "How are you?"

But some people don't say how they really are, not because they're trying to be positive but because they fear rejection if they dared to be open about their pain. Wouldn't it be better if we all could be more real? If we would answer "How are you?" with vulnerability and honesty? Certainly, you'd want to be selective as to who you shared your pain with. Some people aren't a very sympathetic ear. Thankfully, there are many more who are.

So the next time someone asks, "How are you?" test the waters, and share your heart.

Plenty of Time Left

One of my best friends, Mary Scott, is a talented artist. Her work has been featured in juried shows, has won art contests, and received critical acclaim. Her expertise is watercolor, and she's amazing.

Mary is a friend who visits you and takes pictures of your grandchildren, then later sends you an 11 x 14 watercolor of them. Her husband, Don, will take pictures of scenery, and those will eventually end up as Mary's watercolor paintings, too.

The most interesting thing about Mary's art is that she didn't begin seriously painting until later in life. She always knew she had talent, and she always painted, but she didn't pursue her gift until she was nearing middle age.

Another best friend is Linda Aleahmad. She had always wanted to be a therapist, but family life and a family-run business filled her time. But as she neared middle age, she, too, decided to go for it. She went back to school and completed her B.A. degree (she would even go on to complete her Master's), and she opened up two Marriage and Family Counseling offices.

Another good friend, and a woman I call my "adopted" mom, Diantha Ain, put her acting and writing career on hold while she raised her family. Then when she hit middle age, she decided to once again nourish her creative self. In fact, that's where I first met Diantha. And Linda. And Mary. It was in the same writer's organization that we all decided to join to pursue our dreams of writing. Today, Diantha has written a book of children's poetry, numerous articles, original plays and musicals, and her haiku has been featured in books, magazines, and on greeting cards.

Margaret Brownley, another dear friend and fellow member of our writer's group, started writing seriously later in life, too. She's now authored dozens of books, both fiction and nonfiction, hundreds of articles, and has also written for television.

Most of us spend far too much time looking back and regretting the things we didn't get around to doing or pursuing in our twenties and thirties. We think that because we passed on those opportunities, they're gone forever. We think the door has shut on our dreams.

But nothing could be further from the truth. In fact, age might even play in our favor in some creative pursuits. We've lived life, so our stories are richer. Because of our pain and our joy, our paintings can seem more vivid and real. Our music reveals a depth that youth simply cannot bring to the process. Our screenplay characters come to life because we've interacted with nearly every personality known to man. When we write a how-to book, it's because we know how to do something, usually from years of experience.

So whatever dream you think has passed you by, try going for it again. Who knows? Maybe this time you just might catch hold of it.

Stretching Our Days

The older we get, the more obvious something becomes: Life is too short. There simply isn't enough time to do all the things we want to do or go all the places we want to go. Days swoosh by, whole months disappear into thin air, a year runs into the next so fast that you hardly even notice. Before you know it, a whole other decade is behind you, your birthday candles have somehow reproduced themselves, and the person in the mirror staring back at you looks like a wrinkly old stranger.

How do we get it all to slow down? Life sometimes reminds me of that metal merry-go-round at the playground that you would spin faster and faster and then jump on and ride out the revolutions to a dizzying ecstasy. The only way to slow it down would be to drag your foot into the sand alongside it. Sometimes I want to drag my foot in the sand throughout my day. Make the hours pass a little more slowly. I'd like to actually have time to fill in a few pages of my diary before the whole thing is outdated and I have to move on to the next year's. Trees have sacrificed themselves for those empty journals. I feel bad about that.

If you're like me, looking for ways to slow down your life, maybe the following will help. No matter how many more years we may be blessed with, making every day seem at least a little longer can't hurt. Here are few ways to do that:

Ways to Make Time Pass More Slowly

- Get a job at the complaint department of any business.
- Get stuck on an elevator with a life-insurance salesman.
- Join a Whiner's Anonymous group.
- Call a different repairman every day and wait around for him to show up.
- Join book clubs and then try to cancel your membership.
- Spend your day going through your spam file.
- Get all that dental work done that you've been putting off.
- Call a utility company and agree to be put on hold.
- Open a business untangling people's Christmas lights.
- Try programming your universal remote control yourself.
- Go on an extended vacation with an overly opinionated couple.
- Talk to a different cell phone company every day and listen to their sales pitch.
- Rent out your garage to a rock band.
- Attend lectures on subjects you couldn't care less about.
- Seek out people who monopolize conversations, and make them a regular part of your life.
- Sign up for every time-share sales pitch you see offered.
- Take a part-time job at Chuck E. Cheese's.

This is only a start. If you think about it, I'm sure you can come up with many more ideas to make your days seem longer.

None of us know exactly how much time we have left. That's out of our control. But making the minutes feel like hours—or each day seem like a week—is something we could easily do to stretch out these second and third acts of our play.

See you at Chuck E.'s!

We Could All Use a Hero

My husband's uncle was in the Bataan Death March. If you know anything about military history, you know that those who were in the Death March were nothing short of heroic.

My brother was also in the military, serving as a military police officer in the United States Army. My cousin served in the Navy in Vietnam, reenlisting multiple times. My niece served in the United States Air Force, and her husband continues to serve in the Air Force. The son of one of my best friends was a career Air Force major; his wife is an Air Force colonel. Another close friend was a Marine and served simultaneously in the Air National Guard and as a lieutenant in the police force. My husband served in that same police department for almost three decades. Other relatives and friends are military or police personnel, from uniformed officers to Chiefs of Police.

Writing for Bob Hope's USO Desert Storm and Beirut shows, as well as military tribute shows, I've had the pleasure of meeting many of our servicemen and women. I also had the opportunity to read hundreds of letters that soldiers have written to Bob over the years, dating all the way back to World War II.

One of my favorite letters was from a GI who was writing to thank Bob for something special that he had done. It seems that when Bob was appearing in his area, he and his company walked miles to get to the show. But by the time they arrived, there were so many thousands of soldiers already there, they couldn't get close enough to see or hear him. So they turned around and started walking back.

When word of this reached Bob, he gathered a bunch of the stars together after the show, and they drove out to find that company of soldiers along the road. When they did, they parked and put on a private show just for them. This soldier was writing to thank Bob for being a hero to them that day.

There were also letters from countless mothers, each one thanking Bob for the personal phone call he had made to them, delivering greetings from their sons or daughters whom he had met on the battlefields.

That's a hero.

In my book, they're all heroes.

So what makes a hero? A hero, I believe, is someone who puts it all on the line for someone else. Who reaches out in both big ways and small ways to a person in need. Someone who makes a difference in someone else's life, even when there's nothing in it for them—especially when there's nothing in it for them. And they're not always in uniform.

We saw plenty of heroes on 9/11. People who didn't stop to think who was "worthy" of being saved. They simply saw that people were dying, and they risked their own lives to rescue as many of them as they could.

A hero can be that friend who holds your hand and lifts you up during a difficult time in your life and refuses to let go. A person who believes in your best, even when you're not showing it.

A hero can be a doctor, a teacher, a coach, a pastor, a pet, and even that total stranger who tells you that you've got spinach between your teeth or a tag hanging from the back of your shirt.

Heroes can be friends and family who stay by your side at the hospital when your loved one is in ICU. Or the person on the other end of a twenty-four-hour prayer line, who will pray with you for your prodigal son or daughter to come home.

A hero can be the hospice nurse caring for a terminally ill patient, or the Salvation Army worker helping feed the homeless at Thanksgiving.

Heroes can show up when we least expect them. Once, when I was taking my mother to chemotherapy treatments for lymphoma and she was too sick to walk into the medical building on her own, a hero appeared out of nowhere and volunteered to stay with her until I could get a wheelchair from the doctor's office. I hadn't even asked for help. He just showed up and volunteered.

How many times have you been feeling low and then received an encouraging letter or e-mail from someone out of the blue? That's a sure sign of a hero—their timing is always perfect.

If you've gotten this far in life, chances are you've seen your share of heroes. Leaders like John Kennedy and Ronald Reagan, people like Mother Teresa and Danny Thomas, who gave so much of themselves to others. Your heroes may even be members of your own family, who have sacrificed time, money, and resources so you can have a better life. They're all heroes.

Perhaps you've been a hero in someone's life yourself. I'm sure you have. Often we don't realize how many lives we're affecting by our actions every day. It might have been something as simple as a smile to someone who desperately needed it.

The world needs a lot of things today, but it can always use more heroes.

This story originally appeard in New Christian Voices, *www.newchristianvoices.com/column/marthas-laugh-lines-we-could-all-use-a-hero*, August 15, 2008.

Living Life in Reverse

If you spend any time at all watching television, you have no doubt seen the ads touting the advantages of reverse mortgages. They're all the rage right now. But before you rush out and sign over the family farm, you should know that there are plenty of knowledgeable people on both sides of this issue.

Financial guru Dave Ramsey (leading us all through the parted waters to debt-free living) will be quick to say that reverse mortgages are a terrible idea; mortgage companies will charge you high interest rates and outrageous fees.

Reverse mortgage companies and, of course, Robert Wagner will no doubt have a different spin on the matter.

I think I'm going to side with Dave on this one. It does seem like the mortgage companies have simply found another way to get their hands in our pockets. We're finally wising up and getting out of the credit card game, so they've got to go after something else, like our kids' inheritance.

Without getting into a debate on the matter, though, what I'd really like to do is simply look at the possibilities of reverse payment arrangements on other things. Like, for instance, groceries.

Why hasn't anyone come out with a reverse grocery bill? I can clearly see the advantages to this, can't you? If there were a reverse checkout lane where, instead of our paying for our groceries, the grocery store would pay us back for having shopped there all those years, how great would that be?

Or how about a reverse Visa bill? Do you have any idea the kind of money we could make if Visa started giving us back the 10, 15, and 24 percent interest they've been charging us to use their credit cards all these years? Let *us* build the seventy-story high-rises for a change. We could build the mega entertainment arenas and name them after us. Isn't it our turn now?

And what about reverse car payments? After we've paid off our car, why can't the car loan company start sending us a monthly check? How thoughtful would that be? Every month they could just drop a small token in the mail as a thank-you for all the interest we paid them over that five-year stranglehold—I mean, loan—we had with them.

Reverse clothing payments would be good, too. If we're going to be paying on the clothes we buy on credit for twenty or thirty years, couldn't that get reversed at some point—say, when they go out of style—and then the company would start paying us instead?

See, with the right focus, these reverse payment options do have a lot of merit.

Taking Inventory

One good thing about growing older is that everything we own has grown older with us. The toys we had as children are now collectors' items. The baseball cards and comic books we saved (or for most of us, *didn't save*) are now worth a small fortune. The cars we drove have become "classics." Even our old *See Dick Run* books or our *Howdy Doody* lunch pails now command a pretty penny.

The trick was to have had the wisdom to hang on to them. Most of us didn't have that kind of foresight. That's why these items are worth a lot today. Supply and demand. There are a lot more of us baby boomers looking to replace these items in our childhood memories than those of us who actually saved them.

But how do you know which things will one day be valuable and which things won't be? For the most part, it's a guessing game. I've held on to childhood souvenirs that I was sure would increase in value. I've carefully packed them when we've moved, I've guarded them like a museum curator, only to later discover that they're now worth about four dollars.

By the same token, I've gotten rid of things I thought were worthless. Things that I couldn't get rid of fast enough and I thought had no sign of value whatsoever. Of course, these are the same items that I find selling for hundreds—and in some cases, thousands—of dollars on eBay.

I suppose it's like they say: "One man's trash is another man's treasure." And when you get down to it, the rule of thumb should be to keep what has value to you and your family and let go of the rest.

I believe I have every card or drawing my children, and now my grandchildren, have ever given me. These have value to me.

I'm a picture nut and have hundreds of family photos of everything from family vacations to birthday celebrations to tea parties to Little League games and more.

But I also have "stuff." Lots of stuff that I'm hanging on to; things I don't really need and don't have room for. Stuff that's just taking up space or taking attention away from those things I truly want to have around.

So every so often go through your "stuff" and take inventory. If it's something that brings a smile to your face, a warm feeling to your heart, or some other sign that there is an emotional attachment, keep it. If it's something that is on track for having some monetary value, keep it. But if it's the Penney's catalog from 1991 or a restaurant coupon book from the '80s, it's time to start tossing. If the recently enacted airline policy of charging for additional baggage has taught us anything, it's the fact that we tend to travel with a lot more stuff than we truly need. We do that in life, too. So let's go through our houses as we would our luggage and rethink a few things. What do we really need to keep, and what can we leave behind? Traveling through life with a lot less baggage will do us all a lot of good.

Lost and Found

Once, while my family and I were swimming in a nearby lake, the unthinkable happened. We hadn't been swimming for very long when I pulled my hand out of the water and felt my wedding ring slip off my finger. My heart sank. As did the ring. The water was about waist-deep and murky, as lake water often is. I couldn't have seen the Loch Ness Monster in that water, much less a wedding ring.

Now, I should mention that this happened at a time in our lives when we really didn't need any more stress. Problems seem to have that kind of timing, don't they?

I told my husband what had happened, and immediately he and two of our sons began diving down to look for the ring. They couldn't stay down for long on their own, so alternately, I would have to hold them under the water so they could search. Each time they came back up, they were empty-handed.

We searched the dark waters for around an hour. But now the sun was beginning to set, and I found myself having to come to terms with never seeing my wedding ring again. The wedding ring that I had worn since I was eighteen years old. The one that had been through over thirty years of life with me. It had seen several sizings due to weight gain or weight loss; it had been in thousands of sinks full of dirty dishes; it had been lost and then found in laundry baskets and various other places. But now it was somewhere in the sand under several feet of lake water, and probably getting buried deeper and deeper with each step we took.

It was looking hopeless.

Just before giving up, though, something or Someone gave me the thought to look at the current of the water. The ring probably didn't fall straight down. Instead, it must have sank at an angle. But in what direction?

I told my husband that we needed to fan out about four or five feet, and then move in a circle around our original position, searching the sand beneath us for as long as the sunlight held out. If our task looked daunting before, in that small area we were searching, now it looked even more overwhelming.

But I couldn't bear the thought of giving up on this one last chance of finding my ring. So we fanned out and began our new, wider search. Holding on to my husband's shoulder for balance, I reached my hand down and started wiggling my fingers through the sand below. I was determined that we would keep moving around in the circle and cover as much ground as we could until it got too dark to see.

I still can't believe what happened next. In fact, to this day, we're all in amazement. It was the first place we stopped when we fanned out, and I had been feeling through the sand for only a few minutes when I felt something circular and hard. The thought crossed my mind that it could have been a pop top or perhaps even a fish hook. But I wasn't about to let go of it! Carefully, I pressed my finger in the circular portion and slowly brought it to the surface.

When I saw what I had in my hand, I couldn't believe my eyes! It wasn't a pop top or a fish hook. It was my ring!

Now, you would have to know how big this swimming area is, how murky the waters were, and how close the sun was to setting (and how close we were to giving up on the search) to understand what a miracle this was! And it came at a time when we needed a miracle to remind us once again Who is in charge and Who knows every grain of sand and every treasure hiding in murky waters.

And yes, after that, I did get the ring sized.

High Tea, Bowling, and Other Family Traditions

My granddaughters and I have always loved playing tea shop, beauty salon, store clerk, and office. It's one of the perks of being a grandmother: You still get to play. Their shops are pretty realistic. My oldest granddaughter makes out receipts, draws and cuts out pretend money, and goes through my house putting price tags on things that already belong to me. Then she sets up her store and calls us in to go shopping. Or she announces that it's time for my beauty appointment, or tea is served, or the restaurant is open, and so on.

For the tea parties, we often wear hats and use English accents.

After a few minutes in her beauty shop, where customers can get their hair and nails done, or even a facial, my face will sometimes become her personal canvas for all sorts of colorful experiments. (I don't realize this until I look in the mirror.) But it's relaxing.

After the beauty appointment, I will move on to another store or restaurant.

Other members of the family will also get involved by shopping, having a beauty or nail appointment, going to school, eating at her restaurant, or getting their hair styled at the barber shop.

My granddaughter has gone from the grand opening of just one store to the ribbon-cutting ceremony of opening an entire mall in my living room. She's also added the convenience of credit and debit cards, job applications (for the other kids to work at her stores), and P.E. classes for her school.

Grandkids are fun, aren't they?

Another activity that we do in our family is our family bowling league. There are ten of us bowlers, plus twin toddlers. Everyone has their own color-coordinated team bowling shirt with their name embroidered on it. The twins have their own shirts, too, with the words *League Manager* printed on them.

Each week I'll give every player a copy of the league scores and standings, and at the end of the summer, we will even have an awards ceremony and distribute trophies.

We all look forward to our bowling nights, which we can plan at a moment's notice, and it has become a fun family tradition.

It's good to have family traditions. I'm sure you have some of your own. It means you're building memories. And that's something no amount of money can buy, and no recession can take away.

Longevity

I recently read an article in a magazine that said I could add half a year to my life if I would just exercise more. But let's think about this: If I run a mile every day for the rest of my life, which, for the sake of argument, might be thirty more years, that's 10,950 miles—10,957, counting the leap years. Now, forget using an eight-minute mile as a basis. It would take me more like thirty minutes to run that distance. That being the case, we're talking approximately 5,479 hours spent in the act of running. That works out to roughly 228 days, which is a little more than seven months. So the time that I would spend exercising totals seven months—but it only gains me six months. Are you following my logic here? I would lose seven months on the jogging track in order to gain six months of life. That doesn't make mathematical sense, does it? I wouldn't even be enjoying those extra seven months. The incentive just isn't there for all that sacrifice. I'm not getting near enough of a return on my sweat. In fact, by my calculations, I'm losing a month.

But if they changed their calculations to where I'd not only get the extra six months but also a trip to New York, a new car, or some other grand prize, then I might be tempted to take to the jogging trails. But until then, you'll find me in any of my usual places: in front of my television or computer, or asleep on the sofa, using my six months in a far more productive way—living my best nap now.

Next Chapters

Next chapters move a story along. They reveal the internal strengths and challenges of the protagonist. They can provide comic relief, bring new adventures, and make you weep with joy or empathize with the characters.

Next chapters also unveil the identity, as well as the motives and methods—and in some cases, the ultimate defeat—of the antagonist. Sometimes this revelation surprises us. It's not always whom we think it is.

No matter how much our hearts are pounding as we turn the page, next chapters don't always bring us what we feared. Instead, they can twist and turn and surprise us with something wonderful—something we didn't even realize was a possibility.

Next chapters provide perspective. They can bring resolution to problems and tie up loose ends. They can answer our questions from previous chapters or bring us new mysteries to solve. Next chapters can span a passage of time or temporarily revisit a past incident for clarity and the personal growth of one of the characters.

Next chapters are a good thing.

They are a good thing in life, too.

Maybe you've had to face difficult circumstances, such as the loss of a loved one, the loss of a relationship, or the loss of a dream. Your next chapter can mean leaving behind that pain and beginning a brand-new page. A new normal, as they say.

Next chapters can bring us an unexpected plot twist, a change of setting, the introduction of new characters into your life, and a much happier ending.

Who knows what kind of adventure your next chapter is going to bring? Only God knows the outline of the whole story. That's why we keep turning the pages—to find out what kind of choices we're going to make, what twists and turns our plot is going to have, and what we're going to learn in the process. The anticipation of the unknown is exhilarating.

Will we jump ahead of God's best for our lives? Stray from the outline here? Get back on the outline there?

Sometimes a new chapter will bring a flashback. Flashbacks are good to remind us all where we've come from. They show us bits and pieces of our backstory. But we have to be careful not to live our lives in flashbacks. If you spend too much time going from flashback to flashback, you'll lose the forward progression of your life story. That doesn't work in novels or movies, and it doesn't work in life.

Next chapters in our lives don't always bring us what we feared, either. How many times have you been reading a novel and everything is pointing to the hero's certain destruction, but by some miracle the hero survives everything that is thrown at him or her and, by the end of the book, even triumphs. This scenario happens in life, too. We've all heard of people who were given only a few months to live but then go on to outlive their prognosis. My good friend and gifted author Sue Buchanan did just that—plus she outlived the doctor who gave her the prognosis!

She was diagnosed with cancer and not only ended up beating the disease but also wrote a book titled *I'm Alive and the Doctor's Dead.*

When I was first diagnosed with diabetes at the age of eighteen, it felt like a death sentence to me. I had grown up with an older sister who had been diagnosed with diabetes when she was four years old. I recall coming home from school and seeing an ambulance parked in front of our house on many occasions, due to her severe low blood sugar reactions. She had been hospitalized for hyperglycemia many times, too. She did eventually succumb to the disease, after having two toes amputated and developing several other major complications.

So, yes, I wasn't sure what the disease would mean to me.

But now, some thirty-eight years after the original diagnosis, I'm still here. I once calculated that I've had over 38,000 injections in my lifetime. But I've found an advantage to this, too. I can drink a glass of water and then walk through the house and water all the houseplants at the same time.

When actress/singer Ann Jillian was first diagnosed with cancer, she wondered what her next chapter might bring. But then Ann and her husband, Andy, decided to make a fifty-year plan. They decided that they would live their lives for the next fifty years as worry-free as possible. They didn't want to get to the end of fifty years and realize that they had wasted all that time worrying about something that might never happen. They wanted to enjoy each and every day of their lives. And they have. Today, decades after her original diagnosis, Ann is thriving and indeed enjoying her life.

So don't waste the chapter you're in by worrying about what the next chapter might bring. Turn your pages one at a time. Even if you're in a difficult chapter right now, hang on. God knows your whole story. He might be saying, "Yes, chapter 7 has a lot of heartache, but wait until you see what I have in store for you in chapter 8." Or, "If you'll just trust me through chapters 12 and 13, you'll see how it all comes together in chapter 15, and you're going to love how the story turns out in the end!"

Life will always have its ups and downs, its page-turning drama, and hopefully, plenty of comic relief thrown in, too. And no, we don't know what the next chapters are going to bring. But one thing's for sure: If we're still turning pages, it's not the end of the book yet. Our story is unfolding with every chapter, every paragraph, every word. Will our lives be perfect? No. Will our children be perfect? If you think your children will be perfect, you're probably still looking at their sonogram. Will your marriage be perfect? If you've set your bar for a perfect marriage, get back to me after the reception. No marriage, no family, no one is perfect. Why? Because life isn't perfect. We're all going to have difficult chapters to get through. You'll have to interact with characters you don't much care for. You'll have great scenes, and some scenes you'd rather send back for a rewrite.

But if you persevere until the end, one day you will look back on your life story and realize how much you've learned, how much you've grown, and how blessed you are to have lived such an incredible story.